MEETING
JESUS TOGETHER

MEETING JESUS TOGETHER

INTRODUCING
SALUGENIC COMMUNITY

SUSAN B. WILLIAMS & PETER R. HOLMES

Biblica Publishing
We welcome your questions and comments.

USA	1820 Jet Stream Drive, Colorado Springs, CO 80921
	www.authenticbooks.com
India	Logos Bhavan, Medchal Road, Jeedimetla Village, Secunderabad
	500 055, A.P.

Meeting Jesus Together
ISBN-13: 978-1-60657-102-6

Copyright © 2010 by Susan B. Williams and Peter R. Holmes

12 11 10 / 6 5 4 3 2 1

Published in 2010 by Biblica Publishing
A catalog record for this book is available through the Library of Congress.

Printed in the United States of America

We dedicate this book to you:

You are suffering from a disease called sin.
It has isolated you from the person God created you to be,
as well as from authentic relationships with others.

But God already knows this and has provided the answer for you,
so He is now eager to talk to you about you, more willing than you
are probably willing to listen.

He wishes to show you how you can change. Through salugenic
moments with Christ and with others, He invites you to move into a
journey of increasing wholeness,
to become simultaneously more like Christ and more
uniquely yourself.

CONTENTS

Scripture is full of phrases we have become very familiar with, but such familiarity can often hide our ignorance. Think, for instance, of Christ's promise that where two or three are gathered in His name He will be present (Matthew 18:20). Do we really understand what this means? Is it really part of our daily experience? Also, what about the "body of Christ" and our (lack of?) experience of it? In 1 Corinthians 12 Paul describes in some detail what that should be like from God's perspective. So why is our experience so very different?

I (Susan) have always been one to ask awkward questions. My curiosity knows no bounds. But when I was a child, it was significantly quenched by my fear of people. My world did not seem to make sense, yet I did not know how to ask about what was really going on. I retreated instead into being excessively shy and learned how to people-please.

Now, however, I have found freedom from such fear and can be quite unapologetic with my explorations. This book is an adventure into questions far more exciting and significant than I could ever have imagined.

A Personal Comment

My own journey into wholeness was remarkable. I have written about it in *Letting God Heal*.[1] It was a gradual miracle rather than a spontaneous one, a painful miracle rather than a glorious one. But because it happened slowly, I was also able to indulge my curiosity and understand in significant detail how God was healing me. It has been my delight to teach many others how to find their own wholeness as they learn to let God work in their lives in similar ways.

My first nervous breakdown meant that I viewed my relationship with God as scarred by failure. At twenty-one I had been a Christian for six years, but now I found myself seriously ill: I was to remain ill for the next two years. I pulled myself together with the help of medication, friends, and lots of hard work; but several years later, when I was slipping quietly and secretly into my second nervous breakdown, I lost all hope. My previous twelve years of church attendance had included a great deal of Christian leadership, but where had that got me if I was now ready to quit?

I did not expect such a trauma to be the time when I would begin a radically new journey with Christ. I was more ready to give up on life than embark on a life-changing adventure. But God always has surprises for us: that is, when He is able to get our attention. My breakdown was one of these attention-getters!

This book is one of God's biggest surprises for me. I was desperate for Him to intervene in my emotional illness. I knew even then that there was so much more that He intended for me, so much that should be part of the normal Christian life. But I simply did not see the tapestry God was weaving. He has brought together so many dissimilar threads over such a long period of time that I feel as if I have only just seen what in some ways I have always known.

My church history has also been a remarkable thread, sometimes painful yet also wonderful. I have had the privilege of being part of two teams that have planted churches, and I have been in leadership of some sort for much of my Christian life. There have been times when God has met us supernaturally week after week and we have all been changed by His presence. There have been times when I've grieved for the loss of His presence and of what He has wanted to bring.

My academic life has been another thread. Academically, I never expected to continue my studies after my initial degree in sociology. Yet now I find that my research has produced a PhD thesis, among other things, and I am a specialist in creating relationships and communities that help people to change. The Lord wove that thread in without my fully realizing what He was up to.

The relevance of my professional background was again a surprise. My experience of working with people and in organizational management had given me a perspective on change that extended into the world of business, health, and social care. But I have to confess that I viewed it as somewhat separate from the rest of my journey. My consultancy work simply paid the bills. God, however, had other ideas. All that I came to understand about creating more wholeness and ensuring personal development and greater effectiveness in business contexts has also enabled me to learn more about the type of transformative change that God wants all of us to discover.

Discovering Salugenic Communities

It was when I was at my most sick that I first met Peter and his wife, Mary. That was when the weaving really began. That was when my curiosity came to life. Peter was patient with my hunger to learn. As my journey of wholeness unfolded through his ministry, we each spent many hours writing up its biblical framework and practical application so that the many others who were asking for help could also benefit.

It is rather shocking to us now that for the first ten years we continued in the belief that journeys of healing and wholeness were deeply personal. We knew that God could do amazing things and that He intended this to be the norm in the life of every person who sought His help. We taught many how to grow the skills needed in their own relationships with God, how to find the freedom He promised. Yet it was all on a one-to-one basis.

In these last ten years God has taken us on a far more radical adventure. First through Peter's PhD and then through my own, we have explored the centrality of relationships, the body of Christ, and what all this means to our experience of the presence of God in our lives. When God wants to move in wholeness and healing, and we are willing to let Him do this in and through one another, something completely new begins to happen.

This discovery was not simply academic. All our research was based around the church we had helped to plant, Christ Church Deal, in Kent. Early in our history there was such a high proportion of the congregation actively seeking out more of God's healing that He birthed a synergy in our midst. Supernatural wholeness became contagious.[2] The presence of

Christ, when two or three of us were gathered in His name, was consistent and palpable. Those who had no relationship with God were comfortable in our midst, finding wholeness and meeting Jesus when they were ready. This was an adventure in discovering more of the reality of life as the body of Christ.

Our conclusion, as a result of our church experience and our research, is that every time we come together as believers we can know Christ's presence in our midst. We believe that a shared journey of transformative change to increasing Christlikeness, rather than being the exception, can become the norm for life in the body of Christ for any who want to pursue it. One of my examiners for my PhD thesis said that there was a sense in which we had, at that time in the congregation, discovered "paradise," while not realizing what was happening in our midst. The real question, he said, was whether paradise can be intentionally re-created by those who choose to seek it. Our answer, expressed in this book, is, of course, yes! If paradise is the kingdom of God, then paradise is created by the presence of Christ. And He promises that what we seek in His name, we will find.

Susan's Research

(Feel free to skip this section and move on to the next if the foundation of the research is not of interest to you.)

The principles described in this book may seem obvious to some, but this did not stop me from being tempted to put in lots of academic arguments to support these ideas. I rejected this temptation, however, and decided instead to let them speak for themselves, supported by Scripture. But first a few words about how these principles were discovered.

I used a rigorous sociological research method known as "grounded theory."[3] Instead of being rooted in the researcher's preconceptions and ideas, grounded theory uses the ideas and concerns of the participants themselves as the basis for the research: the data directs the research. I held random focus groups with members of Christ Church Deal and then designed a rather long questionnaire. Once I had the data, I began a systematic, computer-assisted analysis to group the findings into codes and groups of codes, known as categories. I found that the theme most prevalent in the data was that of personal change. So this, to my surprise, became the focus of my research.

Relying strictly on the data, I looked at the type of change that was being described, and what contributed to its success. What was the starting point of the change and what was the goal? The participants had not been talking about conversion. Rather, they had been discussing the ongoing personal and emotional growth they had been able to achieve as part of their discipleship journey. As is best practice in grounded theory, I also began to explore the theoretical relationship between the codes and categories, to draw out the principles that might have a wider application.

I also used comparative data from other sources. I did not find much literature in theology and ecclesiology about the type of change my analysis had uncovered. So instead I considered therapeutic community contexts and the field of education. I also moved in the direction of sociological social psychology, looking at the group processes that support change and the interaction between the macro (group) and micro (individual). For instance, how do the context and environment we are in affect our capacity to change?

The most successful outcome of grounded theory research is the development, on the basis of one's analysis, of a new theory about a particular aspect of human interaction. In my thesis I was able to propose such a theory and to set it out in great detail.[4] In my doctoral research, as in this book, I am suggesting the beginning of a new social psychological theory of the formation of community.

Although my initial research was undertaken in a department of theology, I based my doctoral research at the Graduate School of Education at the University of Bristol. Therefore I did not specifically apply my findings to church contexts. In this book, relying heavily on the findings of my research, Peter and I develop the theory further, exploring the subject from both a congregational perspective and a biblical perspective.

Discipleship as Wholeness

This book complements the two books we have already written on discipleship as wholeness. In the first, *Trinity in Human Community*, Peter explored a theology of change in the Godhead, focusing particularly on the ongoing perichoretic relationship between the Father, Son, and Holy Spirit—a mutual pouring of love into one another within the Godhead. We also included a description of how day-to-day church life might be a living reflection of the relationships among the Trinity, using illustrations from our own church experiences.

Our second book, *Becoming More Like Christ*, explored what it means for us to become more Christlike. We suggested that such change is a journey in which we can each individually and proactively participate. Rather than simply being a sovereign work of the Holy Spirit that is done to us, we proposed that in the task of spiritual formation, the onus is on each of us. That is, we can choose to change to become more Christlike. Christ has already told us what we need to do, and most of us resist it.

In this book we go one step further. Based on what God has done among us as a congregation, and also on our wider research and on what is clear in Scripture, we will explore the growth that is facilitated when Christ is in our midst in our day-to-day relationships. We will suggest the kind of change that God wants to bring to each of us and the characteristics of the relationships that will help make that change an ongoing reality. More importantly, we will consider what each of us can do, individually and within groups, to help ensure that the body of Christ becomes more of what God intends.

From time to time throughout the book we will also build specifically on the clues that we have in Scripture, clues that are given us from what happened when Christ was physically present with the disciples and the crowds. We would encourage you to consider turning to some of those passages and meditating on them, inviting the Lord to talk to you about them. You may want to do this after you have read the book, exploring for yourself the contexts in which these ideas are found in Scripture. We are very aware that we have only just begun to open up these ideas in Scripture, and we hope others will want to do much more research than we have been able to do.

We have also taken the liberty of including questions for consideration at the end of some of the chapters. Our hope is that this will not be a book that you will simply read and then put down. We would like you to feel that you want to work hard to apply its concepts very specifically to your own circumstances, to your ministry, and to your relationships. The questions are intended to be a prompt that might help you do this.

Our prayer is that you will be able to use some of the ideas and experiences we describe in this book as a way of knowing more of the presence of Christ in your life. There is an adventure that we are all called to embark on—the adventure of building communities that are full of life-changing encounters with Christ. May God give each of us grace to play our part in becoming the people we were created to be, each of us taking our place in the body of Christ.

Susan B. Williams, Deal, U.K.

Peter R. Holmes, Galveston, Texas, U.S.A.

July 2010

Part 1
WHEN CHRIST IS PRESENT

In our twenty-first-century world, can Christ really be present when we meet together? When He is, what difference does that make to us and in us? We begin our exploration of how to meet Jesus together by considering what God intends to happen when we meet in small groups and in churches.

WHEN CHRIST DIED, ROSE FROM THE DEAD, AND ASCENDED INTO heaven, it was the most amazing and supernatural event the world had ever known or would ever know. Human beings now have the possibility of salvation and eternal life. Words are grossly inadequate to convey the significance of the miracle that God achieved. The creation of the material universe was remarkable enough, but salvation is awesome.

With such a miracle there should not be a "but." Yet there is. Christ's ascension was a pivotal moment—He left earth and returned to heaven. But He left His disciples behind. He had gone. The series of events that began with His incarnation had transformed heaven and earth for all eternity, but they culminated in Jesus departing. Did some of the disciples feel that He had abandoned them?

There is a quick theological response to this question, of course. In one sense, Christ had left the disciples, but His promise was that the Holy Spirit was still to come. He would comfort; He would bring the presence of Christ; He would bring all truth. But let us face it. It is not the same. There is no longer any physically manifest Son of God for us to hear, see, touch, and learn from. Jesus is no longer here to sit and to eat with, to walk with through the olive groves or the shopping mall. Neither can we watch as He heals in His unique and sometimes eccentric ways.

From the simplest of perspectives, Christ, it seems, is gone. First He was gone when the disciples and others watched Him die on the cross, and then there was that amazing experience as they each discovered that He really was alive again. But when He ascended, there was a whole different sense of parting. Another would come, the Holy Spirit, to be their friend and Counselor, to bring them the presence of Christ. And yet, Christ was still gone, wasn't He?

When Jesus walked on earth, the most amazing things happened. All who came to Him for healing found themselves healed. Many discovered a new or deeper relationship with God. They found truth about themselves and others. Day after day they saw the impossible become possible. Surely it is a tragedy when such a Man departs? But—according to the Gospels—this is not a tragedy.

In this book we will suggest that while there is a sense in which everything is now different, it is also true to say that in another sense nothing has changed. There is much that the church can and must recover of the reality of Christ's presence. Let us explain.

CHAPTER 1

"When Two or Three Are Gathered . . ."

Before He departed, Jesus gave His disciples the most incredible collection of promises. At their heart was simply the assurance that "where two or three are gathered together in my name, there am I in the midst of them" (Matthew 18:20, KJV). When they met together, even just a small number of them, they should expect Him also to be there. Although ascended, He would still be with them.

This is a significant promise. At its face value, when taken together with other passages of Scripture, it seems that we, in the twenty-first century, can still expect to know that Christ is present in our midst. We can meet Jesus together. Even though He is not physically present in the way that He was with the disciples, the continued reality of His presence can still be the norm. We do not need to feel abandoned, we are not alone, and others should still be able to look on and know that Christ is among us, just as the disciples knew He was.

What we are describing here is one dimension of the potential supernatural nature of church life. Whenever two or three of us are gathered in Christ's name, He is present. This may be in a worship service or in a small group. It may be in a café or a church building. It may even be among two or three people from different congregations. Whoever participates, whatever the location, when two or three are gathered in His name, Christ is present.

So why is it, then, that for many of us, on many occasions, the reality seems quite different? Often when we meet one another, it really doesn't feel like Christ is there. In a church meeting, we might work hard at reminding ourselves that He is, but when we are really honest, don't we have to admit that there seems more faith than reality in these assertions of His presence in our gatherings? Sometimes we simply forget that we should expect Him to be present. Also, what about those times when, if Christ were physically present, we might be embarrassed about some aspects of what is happening and would want to lead Him quickly away?

The clue to what we have lost comes in Christ's high-priestly prayer in John 17, the prayer He prays just before He is arrested and crucified.

> I in them and you in me. May they be brought to com-
> plete unity to let the world know that you sent me and
> have loved them even as you have loved me. . . . I have
> made you known to them, and will continue to make
> you known in order that the love you have for me may
> be in them and that I myself may be in them.
>
> (John 17:23, 26)

While it is true that Christ is no longer present on earth in the way that He once was, Scripture is quite clear that in another sense He still is. Instead of His being physically next to each of us, He is now in us. Instead of Christ being in the room in bodily form, He is in each one of us in the room. So although in one sense, experiencing the presence of Christ through the ministry of the Holy Spirit is very different from having Him physically present, in another sense, He is still just as present.

Here we have the challenge. Where two or three are gathered, Christ is present in each person through the presence of the Holy Spirit. Each of us is expected by Christ to bring the reality of His presence with us into our relationships with others. This is how we meet Jesus together, but how can we do this consistently?

The church can and must continue to manifest the anointed presence of Christ. This puts the spotlight on the significance of our journey into greater Christlikeness, a journey that we first explored in *Becoming More Like Christ*.[1] We each have the potential, indeed the responsibility, of carrying the reality of the manifest presence of Christ with us and in us, together.

Imagine a community, a small group, or a church where the majority of members have learned how to consistently carry the reality of Christ being in and among them. When they meet together, each person is able to bring the presence of Christ and to share this reality with others in a mutual giving and receiving.

In such times together it would be as if Christ had not left. They would be having life-changing experiences similar to those of the disciples themselves when they had Christ with them.

Throughout this book we will be considering how we can build relationships (communities) that encourage us to carry the reality of the presence of Christ and to share this reality with others. When we come together and are willing to be aware of His presence, there is a lot that changes in us and between us. Let us look at an example.

A Surprise Visitor

Some time ago I (Susan) was invited to give some support to a group of women meeting for the purpose of encouraging one another in their journeys of healing, Christlikeness, and discipleship. Although from several different churches, they knew one another quite well and had been meeting together for several months. Despite this, their meetings were becoming more "formal" and less effective.

When I arrived, it was not difficult to see why they were struggling. Even as they were serving one another tea and coffee before the meeting started, it was clear that they did not trust one another. Several were not feeling loved and honored by the others. People were on their guard and uncomfortable. They showed it in different ways—some were quiet and clearly lonely; others were loud and overbearing. There was some cutting sarcasm underlying the polite behavior.

We sat down, with the chairs arranged in a circle as was their norm. There was some surprise, as there was an extra chair, still empty, even though everyone was present. After a few moments of discussion I confessed to having brought it into the room. I told them that this was the chair where Jesus was going to sit during the meeting, reminding them that where two or three are gathered in His name, there Christ is present.

There was a stunned silence. Several women found tears coming to their eyes. Others felt shame. Some were simply confused. From that moment on, the atmosphere in the room was completely different. The women were suddenly aware of Christ's presence. In that moment their relationships with one another were changed. They said sorry to one another and to the Lord. They began to share more openly and to listen to one another in love. There was little more I needed to say that evening.

Instead of being formal, superficial, and judgmental, the women were able to focus on giving one another love, on being real and vulnerable together and on supporting one another in their journeys of healing, wholeness, and Christlikeness. They rediscovered the very reasons why they had joined the group in the first place; they felt again a oneness together. The reality of Christ's presence, His manifest presence, took priority over the petty fears and opinions that had dominated the beginning of the evening.

What had happened? It wasn't that when they saw the empty chair, Christ suddenly, physically, stepped into the room. Instead, in response to their heightened awareness of Christ's presence, each of the women made an instinctive choice to change. Consciously welcoming the reality of Christ in their midst had a spontaneous impact on their relationships. When they became more aware of the presence of Christ, they felt different, and their treatment of one another was different. Each of them was also willing to be more honest, to drop their guard.

From a biblical perspective, when they were each willing to be more open and more real within themselves and with one another, then the women also began to connect with one another, person to person. This openness to one another allowed the Holy Spirit to move more freely among them, bringing the sweet aroma of Christ, like the perfume filling the house (John 12:3b). In a sense, only broken pots release their fragrance.

We have a word for the type of relationship that the women rediscovered that night. It is "salugenic." We will introduce the word in more detail later, but the simplest meaning is "wholeness-creating." As a result of embracing Christ's presence, the women achieved a dynamic unity whereby each began to enable the others to grow, to move on, to find more of what they were looking for on their own respective journeys. They were able to give life, wholeness, to one another in ways that they hadn't a short while earlier. Meeting Jesus together had helped each of them to become more like Christ.

For the rest of that evening the women experienced a mutual giving and receiving of the radical kind of love that Christ lived. They discovered more of the reality of Christ being in them and with them together. This is the type of relationship that can happen when we welcome the presence of Christ. A stranger joining the end of the meeting would have immediately noticed something different about it. It was because they were meeting Jesus together.

Dropping Your Guard

Carrying the presence of Christ "in" us by the Holy Spirit is not simply a theological concept. It should be an experience that all of us have and can recognize both in ourselves and in one another. But in order for this to happen, there is a precondition. It is not only that we have to learn how to carry the reality of the presence of Christ, but also that we have to learn how to be present ourselves! Too often, at church for example, we turn up, participate in the worship, smile at others, and even drink coffee or support the Sunday school. But often it is only with the superficial side of ourselves. Were we to reveal what we are really thinking and feeling, many times others would see a completely different person. Perhaps we would reveal ourselves to be disappointed, bored, angry, or even rude. Perhaps, if we would really rather not be there, we might end up saying so. Many of us cannot imagine what might happen if we simply turned up and were spontaneously "real" and therefore "present."

One thing is certain. When Christ was present among people, He always required that they be real. He drew the reality and the presence out of them. For instance, look at the way He drew out the truth in His encounter with the woman at the well (John 4:1–26). Likewise, the woman who touched His cloak in an attempt to find healing was required by Christ to declare herself (Luke 8:42–48). In a similar way, Peter had to be publicly honest about how he felt about himself when Christ called him (Matthew 5:18–20). Never was a polite and superficial response acceptable to Christ. Even with the Pharisees, He brought truth to the conversation, requiring that they admit openly what they were thinking privately (Mark 2:8–9).

We are suggesting that even when we are physically present, we may not be present emotionally and spiritually. Many of us feel the need to hide our more personal thoughts and feelings from others under the guise of politeness or self-protection. Phrases such as "keeping your guard up" and "wearing a mask" point to a hidden reality about us that we feel we need to keep out of reach. When we do this, there is a sense in which we ourselves are not fully present. This makes it almost impossible for us to carry and share the reality of the presence of Christ. Giving Christ in this way without giving ourselves is not possible.

Sometimes this hidden part of us is also invisible to us. In our ministry we talk about such matters being "below the water line," indicating that even we ourselves can be deeply unaware of the reality of our inner life. For instance, a person comes to ask for help, but it is quickly obvious to us that they are not present. They are distracted, a little vacant and emotionally remote. So we ask them where they have disappeared to. We point out to them that they are not present, that they have disconnected or retreated. Often they jump with surprise when we first mention it, and spontaneously become aware of and reconnect with a deeper part of themselves. In our ministry we always require people be present when we are with them!

If we are to welcome the reality of Christ's presence in our relationships together, we will need to be willing to be present ourselves: Christ will require that we choose this presence and reality. We must all cultivate the ability to live "in our own wholeness," a term we will explain shortly (see page 17). Our growing capacity to live in the kind of authentic truth that Christ requires will also allow us to know Christ in us and to share His presence with others.

The journey that we take to build this wholeness and to know the reality of Christ's presence together is what this book is all about. The more we each become like Christ, living in our wholeness, the greater our capacity to consistently meet Jesus together. Likewise, the more we meet Jesus together, the more we become like Christ. This dynamic creates salugenic community.

The Difference Christ Brings

What would our relationships look like if we really lived in the truth that Christ is present? In what ways would our behavior be different if we really believed that Christ was present, through the Holy Spirit? What would change if every time two or three of us were gathered in His name we knew that Christ was there among us? It is our view, as authors, that if all of us learned how to accept and live out the simple reality of Christ's presence when we met together, a number of radical things would begin to happen. Christ lived a radical love, preached a radical message, and brought radical change wherever He went. He made it quite clear that we should expect to do even greater things than He did, because He was going back to the Father and would be able to send us His Spirit (John 14:12; 15:26–27). This, it seems, should be our normal Christian life when two or three of us are gathered in His name. It is what happens when He is present.

Of course, having Christ present in this way may be rather different from what we expect. During His life on earth He very often broke the rules, created chaos and confusion, and turned worlds and values upside down. He offended rulers, loved the unlovely, chastised his friends in public, and slept through storms. He lived kingdom-of-God-on-earth priorities. Likewise, the kind of reality that Christ's presence requires of each of us can be very uncomfortable and quite messy. For instance, some of us would have to work hard to be present. Some of us are rarely transparent and honest, and the idea of learning how is daunting. Such counterintuitive practices can be a real challenge. But we should expect nothing less when we are aware that the King of Kings is among us.

Christ always intended that our relationships with one another should be noticeably different from any other relationships. Of course, they would be if He were present in a unique way. Christ was clear that it is by the quality of our love for one another that we will be known as His disciples (John 13:34–35) and that this love is the Father's love for the Son, in us (John 17:26). This is the difference. It will not be our activities or our behavior, although these will indeed be transformed; it will not just be the words we use; rather, there will be a love so palpable, so real and distinctive, that others will know that this love is because of Christ. Throughout this book we will be looking at the qualities that this love carries, and we hope some of these ideas will surprise you.

We are suggesting that there is a connection between three things. First, we must be willing to be real and present with others, with the truth and transparency that this requires. Second, being present ourselves increases our capacity to carry the reality of the presence of Christ. Finally, we can learn to experience together the reality of Christ being present in our midst when we meet together in our twos and threes. That is, Christ in me meets Christ in you, and together we more fully reflect who Christ really is than any of us is able to do on our own.

This book is a call for us all to be more real and present in the reality of our relationships together. By doing so, we can welcome the reality of the presence of Christ in us as we come together. We are going to explore these ideas and look at how we can each play our part in making it more likely that when we are together we can also know the greater reality of the manifest presence of Christ.

CHAPTER 2

Becoming One

The outcome, or the fruit, of our relationships together is referred to often in Scripture. We have seen that Christ's prayer before He surrendered Himself to crucifixion was "that they may be one as we are one" (John 17:22). In the Psalms David is clear that when there is such oneness, the blessing and anointing of God can be more present (Psalm 133). When the women in the example we gave earlier welcomed the truth that Christ was present in their midst, they became one again, united in their commitment to love one another and Christ.

Have you ever wondered why oneness is so important to God? Of course, it is a better witness to God's love if Christians, instead of being divided, are able to love one another. But I (Susan) have always felt that there is something more significant. In this book we want to explore the idea not only that the oneness of a group of people becomes possible as and when they welcome the reality of Christ's presence into their midst, but also that that same oneness is the manifest evidence that Christ is in their midst. At that moment of becoming one, in openness of spirit and heart, something fundamental changes. If we could see more clearly in the spiritual world, it is likely that the difference would be dramatic.

Let us be clear that we are not talking here about a simple prayer in which we welcome the presence of Christ or a declaration that we want to be in unity. This oneness is not created by the repetition of a series of words. Christ does not pay attention to our words alone. He also discerns what goes on in those deeper parts of us, often referred to in Scripture as our "heart" or our "spirit." It is from here that our welcome of Christ must emanate—from the core of our being, in transparent openness.

If we want to welcome the presence of Christ and live in oneness, we must also be willing to be present ourselves, in honesty. Such honesty may already be true for us and God when we are alone and in private. But being that real with others does not seem to come naturally to any of us. Many of us simply do not know how to have relationships at that kind of depth. Or maybe we have just one or two, arranged by appointment, which we can carefully prepare for (and have a measure of control over!). Simply to live transparently in oneness with others in the presence of Christ—is that really possible in any kind of consistent way? Christ clearly expected that it should be possible for us when we are together.

"In" His Name

The women we described earlier were each on a journey of becoming more like Christ by seeking out deep cleansing and healing in their lives from the damage in their pasts. They had practiced being able to welcome Christ together and had experienced the oneness of His presence. They had already learned in their group how to be so present with one another that nothing need be hidden. So when they welcomed Him again, it was a welcome from the very core of their beings. Was Christ present before those women saw that empty chair in their circle? When they had their guard up and were unable to be in openness with one another, was Christ still in them? Of course He was. But they were ignoring His presence and as a result were not in oneness.

We see many examples in the Gospels of people being around Christ, in His physical presence, yet behaving in ways that were selfish and quite counter to His love (for example, Mark 10:35ff.). They might have been in His vicinity geographically, but His presence had not affected their relationships with one another. They remained unchanged by His love. They were not receiving what He gave and were also not giving it to others. They were acting in ways that suggested that they were unaware of His love. In a similar way, the women in the group were at first not allowing Christ to be manifest among them. Christ was there, but they were not allowing His presence to change their relationships. So for them, it was as if He wasn't there. They were not effectively "in" His name and therefore could not experience oneness. Christ is always present with us, but He is not always manifest to us, either personally or together. We have to practice welcoming and living in the midst of such presence.

Sadly, relationships in churches are not often characterized by oneness. There is a focus on "unity" between churches and denominations and even a debate about the theological barriers to that unity. These are indeed important discussions. But do they lead to the type of oneness that God values? Likewise, we may perhaps pay lip service to the importance of being one with our brothers and sisters yet use all kinds of defense mechanisms to avoid allowing them to get to know us closely. Even among those we know, we hold back from giving ourselves fully in the relationships. We judge, undermine, and criticize. We feel unsafe, keep quiet, or perhaps even stay away. Our words may speak love, but in our spirit we carry fear, bitterness, or anger.

The way we feel about others may make oneness intolerable for all parties. Our churches are places where we meet for the purpose of an activity (the service), rather than to express the oneness we could already be living in. Could it be that for much of the time we are not effectively meeting "in His name"? Are we missing out on the potential of being "in Christ" and His being "in us" while we are together? This may mean that even when meeting together, we are not meeting Jesus.

Our suggestion in this book is that when Christians do meet effectively "in Christ's name," a deep oneness results. To love others in the way Christ intends requires radical change. To know within ourselves the love of the Father for the Son (John 17:23) will change us forever. Hence, for the man and woman on the street, it is the quality of the love we have for one another that is the incontrovertible evidence of the presence of Christ (John 13:35).

Many of us simply have to admit that that love is not a daily reality, that that level of change has not occurred in us as fully as God intends. Perhaps we even, unintentionally, resist the change that being close to others would require of us. As a result, perhaps we accidentally resist the manifest reality of the presence of Christ. Is it that we have forgotten that it is Christ who has brought us together and that it is Christ who makes us one together? As authors, we don't think it is as simple as that. Our suggestion is that many of us simply do not know how to create relationships that allow that level of oneness, transparency, and honesty.

We have not learned how to encourage one another to be present and how to carry the presence of Christ together.

Divine Community

In *Trinity in Human Community*, I (Peter) explored oneness from another perspective.[1] I considered the significance of the relationships between the members of the Godhead: Father, Son, and Holy Spirit. When one is present, all are present, because they are one. They live in uninterrupted harmony, a divine oneness. The members of the Trinity are each giving to and receiving from one another continually. They are in harmony, three and yet one. They each contribute uniquely to the oneness they share and do so without competition. This dynamic is known as perichoresis.[2]

I suggested that part of God's intention for the church is that it should be an expression on earth of the perichoretic relationships of the Trinity. The mutual giving and receiving of the persons of the Trinity can to some degree be lived out in the dynamic of the interaction of our day-to-day relationships. This is what we should expect to happen when Christ is present. When we achieve this manifest presence of Christ relationally with others, we experience "heaven on earth," the kingdom of God among us. This is the presence of the Trinity in unity with us together, manifesting the glory of Christ on earth. Oneness is a reality, especially in the sense of God being in and with us. Christ, together with the Father and the Holy Spirit, is present in our midst; and He is manifest in us when we live this way together.

The difficulty, however, is that living in the perichoretic oneness of divine community does not come naturally to any of us. Even after many years in the church we may be no more able than we ever were to be present ourselves or to live out the reality of Christ in us with others. The supernatural dynamic of mutual giving and receiving may be something we have never experienced. It may even be something we fear. Do we really want to be present with others and with Christ in this way? For instance, will the reality and honesty He requires lead us to experience hurt or perhaps to hurt others? Will it demand more than we are able to give? Also, should we want to begin, where would we start?

Growing Christlikeness

When the women embraced the reality of Christ's presence, they found that their divisions, their suspicions, their barriers were all dismantled in the oneness they found. In that moment, they changed. How they felt when they were arriving or drinking coffee was quite different from how they felt once they were sitting together with Christ in their midst. The change they experienced may have been temporary. When they left, perhaps they were not able to continue living in the freedom that they had tasted while together. But if they were able to come together in this way consistently over a number of weeks, meeting Jesus as they met one another, the change they had experienced would begin to have a deeper impact in their lives. In their oneness, by being together and aware of Christ's presence, they would grow in their journeys toward greater Christlikeness, and the occasional changes experienced when they met together would become more consistent.

This outcome should not surprise us. When Christ was with His disciples, they knew it. Life-changing things happened. Perhaps they found physical healing or discovered what it was to be forgiven for the first time. Perhaps they discovered truth that was life changing, or they moved on in their relationship with God. Maybe they found acceptance from others because of Christ. Whatever the area of growth that Christ brought, the disciples were changed because they had been with Him. People were always different after meeting Christ. Some were changed for the better, others for the worse, as a result of having made decisions either for or against Him. They learned new skills or new things about themselves and found new priorities, or they turned from Him.

The same is true for us today. Being around Christ should mean that we grow and positively change. We should expect life-changing things to happen both to us and to those around us. This will include an increased capacity to be present ourselves in relationship with others, living in openness and authenticity. It will result in a radically new capacity for loving others, which allows us to be in oneness in Christ's presence. We will know that we carry Christ in us and that He will be manifest as we put Him first. We will begin to play our part in the perichoretic giving and receiving that is an expression of divine community.

During the course of our ministry we have come to interpret this idea quite simply. Being with Christ together makes you more whole.

Knowing Christ, growing in Christlikeness, increases your wholeness. Christ, who is the agent of creation, continues His work of re-creation in each of us, gifting us with ever-increasing wholeness. The change this requires in us is our ongoing journey toward greater Christlikeness. It is our becoming more of the person we were created by Him to be. It is our being willing to be real and then to allow others, together with the Father, Son, and Holy Spirit, to be a means of our growing in the wholeness that is Christlikeness.

Introducing Salugenic Relationships

In our research we found ourselves looking for a word or phrase that would describe the relational dynamic of increasing oneness and ongoing change that leads to greater Christlikeness. After exploring a number of areas, we both concluded that the most appropriate term was a word first used by Professor Howard Clinebell in the 1960s. As professor of pastoral psychology and counseling at the Claremont School of Theology, U.S.A., Howard Clinebell developed the concept of "salugenic" ways of relating—relationships that "nurture wholeness and healing."[3] He contrasted these with pathogenic relationships, which are "sickness-producing and growth-blocking."[4] Later he defined *salugenic* as "health- and growth-producing."[5]

The word "salugenic" comes from two words: the Latin *salus*, which means "good health" or "salvation," and the Greek *genesis*, which speaks of the beginning, creation, generation. Something is "salugenic," therefore, if it contributes to the creating of well-being and wholeness. This seems to be a good way of describing Christ's presence and the impact of His life here on earth. He lived salugenically. He inspired more wholeness in every situation where it was welcomed. Likewise, simply by being together in twos, threes, or more, with Christ in our midst, we can have salugenic relationships. At these times God's work of increasing well-being and wholeness takes place naturally, giving an increasing abundance of life.

In our consideration of *salus*, we have to be clear, of course, that the perspective on health and well-being that we are assuming is God's and not the world's. Our Western world has medicalized and individualized the meaning of health, reducing it most commonly to the physical, the personal, and the private. In our work we use a much broader understanding of healing and health, more helpfully captured in the word "wholeness." Scripture suggests that from God's perspective, our wholeness includes relational health, emotional health, and spiritual health. It is a dynamic health, which continues growing in us throughout our lives, rather than something we achieve at some point, after which there is no further development.

Something is whole when it is restored to be what God created it to be. He is the source of all wholeness, as He is the source of all life. Because of the Fall, we are all much less than we were created to be, having all become damaged and tarnished by sin. Our wholeness lies in our being reconciled to God. We then have the potential to become the men and women we were created to be. We suggest that we do not need to become more spiritual, but to become more human.[6] We need to discover the dignity of divinity in our humanity, the way God intended it to be. That is our ongoing journey of wholeness: it is the journey of becoming more ourselves as we become more like Christ.

We are also using God's perspective on salvation. We are not suggesting that salvation is something we earn, something we achieve as we work harder to change. Christ has given us all eternal life; it is His gift to all who are prepared to surrender and honor His name. We can do nothing to earn our salvation. But God expects ongoing positive change from every one of us, for if we are not willing to change in positive ways we will never become more like Christ. This is the part of our salvation that we must "work out" (Philippians 2:12).

In Becoming More Like Christ we described this journey in some detail, suggesting very simply that as we become more mature in Christ, we also grow in wholeness, and that as we grow in wholeness, we become more mature in Christ. These are journeys toward Christlikeness, the ultimate goal of all spiritual formation. Whether we are pursuing healing, wholeness, or discipleship, we are discovering more of who we were created to be and also the image of God in us. Growing in our own wholeness is growing in Christlikeness. Becoming more of the person we were created to be means becoming more like Christ.

Salugenesis—the generating of greater wholeness—is a powerful concept. Christ is the agent of creation and continues His work of birthing more of God's image in us. But the expectation and, indeed, the injunction of Scripture is that rather than simply being a private, even secretive, journey, this is to be shared. We journey together. We are one body, with each part growing into more of Christ and thereby bringing more of Christ to every other part of the body. Being in wholeness means also living in oneness with others.

The impact of such relationships among us is clearly laid out in Scripture. We will "spur one another on toward love and good deeds" (Hebrews 10:24) and encourage one another when we meet together (v. 25). We will "mourn with those who mourn" (Romans 12:15). More significantly, we will know that we are one body, made up of a number of unique parts, each one of worth and to be honored, so that all have equal concern for one another (1 Corinthians 12:21–26).

So this should be our goal, the purpose and fruit of our relationships together. We want to build salugenic relationships—relationships that are effective in spurring one another on in greater Christlikeness. In these relationships Christ is present and actively continuing His work of inducing greater wholeness in all of us. As a result of this we can therefore also live in oneness as the body of Christ with a love that is visible to others.

Maturity Means Relationships

The question that we are addressing in this book is: How can these relationships be built? How can we achieve relationships of this quality, where Christ is effectively in our midst, where a supernatural oneness is then visible, and where increasing wholeness is created? The women's group we described had experienced this type of relationship and then, for a number of reasons, had lost that dynamic. My (Susan's) meeting with them enabled it to be restored. But how can we build such relationships for the first time?

In this book we don't just want to explore the theory. We will make a series of suggestions so that each of us can practice creating these relationships and discover what happens when we meet Jesus together. We will also suggest ideas for growing in our capacity to be real in our relationships with one another, that the wholeness that is Christlikeness can be more present in each and every one of us.

At this stage let us make a simple and perhaps obvious point: salugenic relationships are not for a select few "super-Christians." Rather, they are for everyone. When Christ made His "where two or three" promise, He did not say, "Where two or three women are gathered . . ." Nor did he say, "Where there is a leader present . . ." This promise is for any two or three who meet in His name. Our work has illustrated this. Some of the most effective salugenic relationships we have seen are among men who commit to a deeper honesty and level of mutual support than they have dared to expect elsewhere. It might be more customary for men to project an image of independence, but like all of us, what they need are relationships that propel them into a continual growth to become more of the people God created them to be. For all of us, this means being in relationships where Christ is in our midst.

In *Trinity in Human Community* I (Peter) admitted to a problem regarding the place of relationship in my discipleship journey. I admitted that I saw community relationships as being more for those who were weak, sick, or fragile. My idea was that I would be most whole, most mature and Christlike, when I could live without needing anyone else. How wrong could I be! I had allowed my assumptions to influence my interpretation of Scripture. Like others before me, I had brought my negative beliefs to my reading of Scripture, giving me the outcomes I wanted, rather than what Scripture actually said. Scripture is clear that as we grow in Christ we grow in the interdependence of relationships within the body of Christ. Just as Father, Son, and Holy Spirit are in unbroken relationship with us, so we are designed to be whole and Christlike only in relationship. When any of us are living an I'm-fine-without-relationships kind of false maturity, we have strayed far from the image of God in us. Likewise, when we claim to love the Lord but want nothing to do with other Christians or the church, then we are denying the essence of our faith and our duty to be more like Christ. From God's perspective, in both instances we are deceiving ourselves and have slipped into unreality.

In our ministry we have seen salugenic relationships formed as people have met for the first time and simply spent a weekend together. But salugenic relationships can also happen with those who have known one another for many years. We have watched family life being turned into salugenic relationships, and we have seen the same transformation in church groups. Where any two or three choose to embrace Christ's presence, the reality of the Godhead brings a radical change to the nature of those relationships, as well as to each participant. Something new is created by our being with Jesus and with one another, and increased oneness is part of the outcome.

What is even more significant is that these types of relationships are particularly attractive to those who don't know God. Once we have achieved them and are able to live in them, others seek them out and want to be part of them. We have watched as those without any church background, and often without any recognized hunger for God, have been loved into His kingdom by their participation in relationships where Christ is present in this dynamic way.

Later in this book we will also be suggesting that in salugenic relationships people can welcome the presence of Christ without realizing that it is Christ they are welcoming. Scripture is clear that everything good comes from God (1 Timothy 4:4; James 1:17, etc.). When the goodness that is God is embraced by groups of people, regardless of the context, they are, often unintentionally, inviting the presence of Christ into their relationships.

Salugenic relationships, however, are not what everyone wants. Many find them too authentic, too honest, too provoking. They are not the type of relationship in which you can remain complacent and refuse to change. We are each changed by each encounter with the other and with Christ. Surely it has got to be so? For without such change, what significance has there been in our coming together? Not everyone is ready to commit to this type of relationship and journey with others. But if you are one of those who is seeking this type of relationship, it is our prayer that in this book you will find some clues about how to play your part in increasing the frequency of such salugenic happenings. Likewise, if you have the responsibility of helping others do the same, we would like this book to be a resource in your ministry.

CHAPTER 3

In Summary

When Christ was physically present on earth, there were thousands who were so drawn to Him that they traveled for miles to hear Him, to touch Him, to be in His presence. All who sought healing were healed; that was true for everyone. But He also demanded change. He required people to move into deeper honesty, and as they did so, they found life-changing truth in Him.

Christ expected this to continue happening when He was no longer physically present. Father, Son, and Holy Spirit will make their home with us (John 14:23). The Trinity will be in us and us in them (John 14:23–27). We will be one with them, just as they are one (John 17:20–23). When we meet together, we will know His presence in our midst. These are not just theological statements. Christ expects them to be the bread and butter of our daily life, full of meaning and experience.

Our oneness with God will be most fully expressed when we are one with one another. The perichoretic dynamic of the giving and receiving of divine community will be birthed in us. We will have a supernatural capacity to love others because we have been changed by Christ. When we are living in that oneness, we will know the reality of Christ's manifest presence. Our love for one another will be clear evidence to the watching world that we are His disciples (John 13:35).

These are salugenic relationships. These are the backbone of salugenic communities. Such relationships are not going to come naturally to us. We will each have to commit to a level of honesty that is perhaps initially uncomfortable, honesty with ourselves, with God and with others. But in the resulting journey we will together discover more of the reality of Christ's presence. We will become more like Christ and have a greater capacity to consistently meet Jesus together.

Part 2

TRANSFORMATIVE CHANGE
TOWARD CHRIST

Meeting Jesus together requires change and results in change. In the next three chapters we will explore the impact we can expect this change to have on us. What does it look like, and, most importantly, how can we build relationships that make this change more possible?

THROUGHOUT ALL OUR BOOKS WE HAVE ONE UNDERLYING MESSAGE. Our ongoing relationship with God and our discipleship journey mean a process of continual change, of ongoing wholeness to become more like Christ. This is what God expects, and this is what God requires, from us all. Therefore our message is very specific. When we meet Jesus together, we will each grow in our Christlikeness. This is what will happen when we are gathered in our twos and threes "in" His name. We will each be changed; we will each move on, and continue on, our ongoing journeys of becoming more Christlike. This will also create an increasing oneness with others who are on the same journey. When we adopt this attitude, it will fundamentally affect the type of relationships we have together. These will not be relationships that offer an unconditional protection of the status quo, nor the kind of casual acquaintance that might occur occasionally when it is convenient to us.

Scripture speaks with a focus on a purposeful, disciple-making life through the creation of faith communities made up of those who desire to live the kingdom of God in their midst. Such a way of life demands that we be willing to be "real" with ourselves and with one another and that we each seek greater Christlikeness.

Within Protestant traditions, it has been the emphasis of the church that the change that makes us disciples of Christ comes prior to, or at the moment of, conversion.[1] This is the time when we are born again, when we know for the first time what it is to receive God's love. For some of us, the few months after conversion can often also be a time of adjustment as we change to fit in with the expectations of those who have introduced us to Christ and those who lead the churches we join. After this initial period of adjustment, however, things settle down.

Yet this is not what we see in Christ's ministry. Even just before He ascended, Christ was still working hard to bring increasing change in the lives of His disciples (for example, Thomas, John 20:24–29; Peter, John 21:15–23). At Pentecost that rate of change increased exponentially as the disciples met the risen Christ and began to see more clearly the task He had set before them. Likewise, throughout the New Testament we see numerous examples of purposeful relationships that were bringing change to all who participated. In fact, you would struggle to find a page of Scripture that does not speak of God seeking change in people and nations.

We are suggesting that salugenesis, change that brings the increasing wholeness that is Christlikeness, is at the heart of all relationships where we consciously choose to meet Jesus together. Indeed, if we want to live in oneness and to know the reality of Christ's presence in our relationships together, then we also have to know how to welcome salugenesis. The emphasis of this book is that God intends this change to happen when we come together in His name. We will be looking at the type of relationship that helps precipitate such change. But to build relationships that best enable this type of change, we first need to have a clear understanding of the change that we are seeking to embrace.

We often instinctively treat processes of personal change like a black box. We know what someone was like before they changed, and we can see who they have become after the change. What happens in the middle, however, the processes of change, can be a bit of a mystery. Based on a combination of our own research and evidence from Scripture, we want, in the next few chapters, to untangle that mystery. When each of us understands in more detail the type of change that Christ's presence will unleash, we can better understand how to build relationships that can support these change processes.

Salugenic change will produce more Christlikeness in our lives. For many of us this will mean that areas of damage from our history will be healed. For some the journey will include healing that has a therapeutic emphasis, a letting go of pockets of personal toxic pain and trauma. For all of us the journey will increase our understanding and experience of who God is, as well as our capacity to love and serve Him. There will be a process of profound change as we commit to becoming the people we were created to be and to growing in Christlikeness in order to achieve this. There is another type of change that is talked about in Scripture. It is our journey of dying to the world, as on a cross (John 11:16). For some this is one of the most important aspects of our walk with Christ, and we agree that it has a place in Scripture and the Christian life. But this "cruciform theology," as it is sometimes called, can suggest our being absorbed into God, or losing ourselves in Him. What we are outlining is something quite different. Instead of eliminating our selves for Christ's sake, the journey we are describing is our fulfillment as people made in His image. There is suffering involved, and we will return to this later in the book, but we see the priority from God's perspective as one of Him first giving us the life and wholeness He intended us to know.

In the remaining sections of part 2, we will outline the first three of five characteristics of the change process stirred up when we meet Jesus together. To begin with, we are focusing on how this change impacts us personally. With each idea we will consider the implications that it carries for the quality of our relationships together. How can we create relationships that will make this type of change more likely? What will our salugenic communities look like when they are successfully achieving this type of change?

The type of change that Christ's presence brings we are calling "transformative" change. It is a change that doesn't simply re-form who I already am, making me into someone slightly different, but instead adds something fundamentally different, making me into someone who previously I was not. It is a change that brings the wholeness that is Christlikeness.

CHAPTER 4

Inner Change

The first characteristic of the type of change Christ brings is that it occurs at the core of our personhood. Rather than simply being a change in our thinking, or our behavior, it emanates from the deepest inner parts of who we are. This is why we simply cannot continue to be superficial when we welcome the salugenic reality of the presence of Christ. He calls to the hidden part of us that is at the core of our being.

Contrasting the outer and inner parts of who we are has its disadvantages. It can create the impression that the inner is more significant, more important to God. It can lead us to despise the day-to-day parts of our lives—our appetites, our family commitments, and our employment. In our ministry we emphasize the opposite. Every part of our life has the potential to be redeemed and to become more Christlike.

It is true, however, that this inner part of us does need specific attention. It is the aspect of our personhood that we tend most frequently to ignore. Many of us get so caught up in the visible and immediate aspects of our material world that we forget that we are also spiritual beings, God breathed, and carrying His Spirit in our lives. Some of us struggle to connect with this part of ourselves, and some of us fear what we will find if we make such a connection. Yet the kind of change that Christ provoked in those who met Him often focused around those parts that were hidden to themselves and from others. We should expect no less when He meets us.

Healing in Our Spirits

Scripture has a variety of words to describe this inner part of us. Most common, especially in the Hebrew Scriptures, is "spirit," or *ruah*. Genesis 2:7 describes how we were created from the dust of the earth (our bodies) and the breath of the Almighty (our spirits). The spirit is that nonmaterial part of us that, according to Scripture, will continue living after the body has died (Psalm 31:5; Matthew 27:50; 1 Corinthians 5:5, etc.).

"Soul" is another word used to describe this nonmaterial part of who we are. Theologians debate the difference between the use of the words "spirit" and "soul" in Scripture. For our purpose, however, we are simply going to talk about the deepest and most fundamental part of who we are, which has a significant influence over our whole being. Following Genesis 2:7, we will refer to it as our human spirit.

In our teaching we often talk about our human nature having two levels or aspects. We liken it to a boat floating in the water. Part of our nature is seen by us (for example, our physical body, above the water line), while part of our nature is not seen by us because it is below the water line (for example, our spirit and our feelings). Much of what we are and do is driven by scripts and schemas hidden below the water line. It therefore takes considerable effort for us to learn what is "driving" us. Just as the disciples discovered, our awareness of Christ's presence and our relationships with others often bring to the surface many of these hidden motives and hidden drives.

We may feel that it would be nice if the God-breathed spiritual part of us remained untouched by and immune to our damaged and fallen world. This is a view that was commonly held by ancient Greek thinkers. But when they frowned on the physical and saw the spiritual as a perfect reflection of reality, they were creating a dualistic understanding of the world. Despite the more holistic Hebrew ideas in which the church was born, it was these dualistic, pagan attitudes that won the day in the early church. They gave Christianity an imbalance, favoring the spiritual while disdaining the material. So we see in the early church a setting aside of the physical and material parts of our life in order to pursue the supposedly untarnished and more mystical spirituality of God's world. The twenty-first-century church is seeking a more biblical, holistic, and balanced combination of physical and spiritual reality.

Although our spirit has the potential to know God, and, in knowing

Him, to have eternal life (John 17:3), Scripture indicates that this part of us is also vulnerable, like the rest of our nature. It can be crushed (Psalm 34:18), grow faint (Psalm 77:3), or be troubled (Daniel 7:15). In fact, from God's perspective, every part of our being, including our spirit, has been impacted by the sin and damage of the world we live in. Escaping such damage is as impossible as living in a sewer and smelling nice. Merely being human and being alive mean we suffer damage.

Scripture is also clear about the consequences of damage in our spirit. When it is crushed, poisoned, broken, or simply deceived, it affects our emotion, our behavior, and our body (for example, Psalm 73:21–22). The Lord promises to save those whose spirit is crushed (Psalm 34:18) and to birth our spirit by His Spirit (John 3:6). Such promises speak of the radical change that is needed at the core of our being, below the water line. From this perspective, therefore, any change that God wants to give us must also involve this inner or below-the-water-line part of us. If we try to change our behavior, but do not also seek to bring about change at this deeper part of our nature, we will leave part of the damage intact. Our Christlikeness will then be only superficial, our wholeness incomplete, and our ability to be one with others limited. In Scripture Christ speaks about the human heart (Matthew 5:8, 28; 6:21; 11:29, etc.), in biblical usage often synonymous with spirit, and our need to change at this deep, hidden level, if the change is to be authentic and long lasting.

Digging Deep

Outside the church this message of healing and positive change at the core of our being, or from our spirit, is a message rarely heard. That is partly because of the problem of terminology and partly because there are many who simply do not believe that such change is possible.

A phrase such as "human spirit" has a depth of meaning behind it, revealed in Scripture, though sometimes in such profound ways that we struggle to understand. Outside the church many recognize the reality of a part of us that is other than our body. In social psychology, Melucci's "inner planet" is a useful concept.[1] Likewise, the term "personal identity" is sometimes used to refer to our sense of a self that is more personal than the self that we might project to others.[2] Again, postmodernity recognizes the immanence of spirit and the need for all of us to be more spiritually aware.[3]

Regardless of terminology, however, we find that very little is written about how we can and how we do change in this part of who we are. In psychology, the focus is often more on a change of behavior or on our growing an understanding of what must change. In psychotherapeutic work, though much of the emphasis is on understanding deeper feelings, the change that is sought is often a change in symptoms, rather than the more profound change that is needed below the water line. Talking cures, therefore, also have little expectation of transformative change.

Where this type of significant change is recognized, it is highlighted as rare, and the exception, and frequently as having an element of mystery, rather than as a fundamental opportunity for all of us. It is described as "a deep change," "a profound change" or even "a quantum change."[4] It is little understood and is rarely achieved intentionally or consistently. Yet we are suggesting that this is the type of transformative change that Scripture suggests should be part of the normal Christian life, a natural occurrence as part of meeting Jesus together.

There is significant evidence in Scripture that Christ intended His relationship with His followers to impact the core of their beings. His criticism of the Pharisees, for example, was that they focused far too much on appearances and outer behavior. "These people honor me with their lips," He said, "but their hearts are far from me" (Mark 7:6). Christ requires of all His people that their worship should be "in spirit and in truth" (John 4:24).

God is spirit; and the Holy Spirit, the Spirit of truth, is with us forever (John 14:16–17). When God comes to make His home with us (John 14:23), it seems inevitable that this should change us from our spirit—from below the water line—and then overflow into all areas of our lives. This change is spelled out very clearly throughout Scripture. For instance, Paul contrasts our sinful nature with the fruit of the Spirit (Galatians 5:16–26). The natural fruit of our nature is often anger, selfish ambition, hatred, and drunkenness, etc. But the fruit of the Spirit in us is love, joy, peace, etc. This change, therefore, is not simply an outer clothing covering our dark nature. It is not a superficial way of relating that hides what we really think and feel. Instead, it is fruit that emanates from the core of our being, following change at the core of our being. Such freedom and its fruit are what we are able to live when we are being most real, most transparent, even in relationship with others.

God searches this secret, hidden, below-the-water-line part of us (Proverbs 20:27). He wants to give us "the Spirit of sonship," in contrast to a spirit of fear (Romans 8:15). He is committed to bringing to the surface that which is hidden (Matthew 15:18ff. etc.) so that it can be brought into the light and dealt with (Matthew 18:35; 1 Corinthians 15:25, etc.). This is a process of change deep in the hidden parts of our nature, where we, without God's help, rarely achieve such profound transformation.

This exercise is not only God's work, but also ours. We are required to dig deep, to find the rock solid enough to build on, rather than constructing a most magnificent house that merely pretends to have a good foundation. If our foundations are absent or inadequate, our house will be washed away in the storm (Luke 6:46–49). It is our responsibility with Christ to set aside such vain appearances and instead ensure that that which can't be seen is as solid and magnificent as that which is visible.

It is clear, therefore, that this core part of who we are, our human spirit, has to change if we are to grow in Christlikeness and see long-term consistent change in all areas of our lives. What is hidden below the water line, the root of who we are, must impact every other part of our lives. Yet if our roots are in contaminated water, however hard we try to produce abundant fruit, something will always be wrong. Jesus was clear: "The good man brings good things out of the good stored up in his heart" (Luke 6:45).

Implications for Relationships

Exposing and bringing change to the inner part of a person, that part of us below the water line, is one of the things that characterized Christ's ministry. For this very reason we can expect that when we are gathered with others in His name, this same type of change should be the norm for our lives. We believe that He wants to bring to all of us the transformative change from the core of our beings that is essential if we are to grow in Christlikeness. Such deep change represents a significant challenge to our relationships together. It means that we need to allow others to help us connect with this "inner" part of who we are—we have to be "real," rather than hide the reality of who we have really become. It sounds obvious, even simple, but the truth is quite the opposite.

Much of our "inner" life is hidden, even from ourselves. Which of us welcomes the prospect of other people helping us discover this hidden and sometimes dark part of "me"? Others of us have made a conscious choice to hide such parts of ourselves, perhaps because of the pain or shame that is buried there. Others of us have just a vague feeling of apprehension at what we might discover were we to "dig deep." The majority of us are far happier merely living a compartmentalized kind of life, where the inner, below-the-water-line life is withheld or hidden from us by us. Perhaps we have even been taught that this is more responsible, more mature behavior. What we don't know, can't hurt us . . . or can it?

If we must engage in a process of exposing these deep inner parts of ourselves as part of our journey toward greater Christlikeness, the most common instinct is that it is safer to do it in privacy, alone with God. Surely He can bring these changes in our personal walk with Him without involving others? If we need expert help, we can turn to a confidential, one-to-one relationship with a pastor, a leader, or perhaps even a professional counselor from outside the church. This feels far safer. Then, when we are changed, when we have privately put matters right, we can start being real in relationships with others, right?

Rather shockingly, God's perspective is in fact the opposite. We first have to let others in to the reality of who we really are, hidden deep in our spirits. By allowing others to see the parts of us we are most ashamed of, we see them more clearly, too. And as we let others in, so we let God in. The digging begins.

The instinct to shut others out can deprive us of one of the most amazing outcomes of the presence of Christ among us—the change that He offers. We are denying ourselves the privilege of letting Him bring deep inner change to us through others. Likewise, we are denying ourselves the privilege of letting Him use us in the journeys of inner change undertaken by others. For if we are not willing to take up the challenge of sharing with others our own personal need for deep inner change, then we do not have the right to expect Him to use us in bringing this change to others. We are restricting our experience of the reality of the anointed presence of Christ in our midst.

In order to be fully present in the presence of one another and Christ, in order to fully meet Jesus together, we have to be ready to let others draw to the surface what is below the water line. We should expect that the change God wants to bring will expose and heal the deepest parts of our nature in our spirits. Jesus cautioned us not to throw pearls before swine. In just the same way, in our ministry we do not encourage people to make themselves vulnerable by sharing that inner part of themselves with lots of others. In this book, however, we are exploring how relationships can be built that can welcome Christ's presence. We will be considering how to do this safely, by introducing you to some of the supernatural consequences that can occur when these relationships begin to be formed.

To Consider

- How would you describe that core, or inner, part of yourself? What are the factors that have caused it to become the way it is?
- Describe some of the areas of your life that are still below the water line.
- In what way would you like this to change?
- What experiences have you had of temporary or long-term change in your spirit, or the core of your being? What effect did they have on you?
- What do you fear might happen if you were to begin sharing your inner self with a small group of people?

CHAPTER 5

Affects the Whole Person

When Christ touches our lives, in addition to bringing a change at the core of our being, He will profoundly impact the whole of our personhood. In contrast to the teaching of some contemporary forms of therapy, every part of who we are will be affected. When we are changed by God, the change will not just be cognitive, limited to our thinking.

When the deepest areas of our lives are cleansed and transparent, our whole being will be healthy. When the Spirit of life is resting at the core of our being, everything about us has and will be changing. Scripture describes this as being "born again," as the Holy Spirit giving birth to our spirits (John 3:3, 6). We are a "new creation" (2 Corinthians 5:17), in reality, rather than notionally. This is as a result of change in us that is both radical and all-embracing.

In fact, using the understanding of human makeup that Jesus would have been most familiar with, there are no discrete or separate parts to us. For instance, everything that happens to us in one part of our nature will impact everything else. Scripture extends this truth even further by pointing out that everything that happens to an individual Christian will also impact others who are part of the body of Christ (1 Corinthians 12:12–26). Not only is no one part of us separate from another part, but no one Christian is independent from others.

In marked contrast, many of us live lives that are quite segregated. We act as though we can do anything, anytime, anywhere, without consequences either to us or to others. We also often try to keep each area of our lives separate from other areas, maintaining each in its own separate box. For instance, there are our work lives, our family lives, and our church lives. Then there are our hobbies, our attitudes, our obsessions, and perhaps even our various addictions. But transformative change cannot be limited to any one area, to any one box in our lives. It must, by its very nature, overflow from one into another because it will first emanate from the core of our being, probably from below the water line, from that inner part of us that is present in all these diverse environments. Such deep change brings a greater continuity of personhood throughout every area of our lives, to all aspects of our day, and for as long as we live.

We do not believe that we are stating anything new here. All of us know that if we are to grow in Christlikeness and to live in wholeness, Christ must be present in every aspect of both who we are and who we are becoming. But this means that we must expect uncomfortable, profound, and deep change. When it occurs, it will ripple through every aspect of our lives and fundamentally impact all of our relationships. To illustrate this important point, let us focus on four areas: our emotion, our behavior, our thinking, and our will.

Our Emotion

Scripture is full of references to emotion and its feelings, both human and divine. What the Bible shows is that when we are changed by God in the way we are describing in this book, our feelings will also profoundly change for the better.

I (Susan) used to wrongly assume that it was our circumstances that changed once we were in Christ. If God was blessing the practicalities of our daily lives, then, I thought, it would be easy for our emotion to follow. Living in peace and joy will, of course, become a reality when things are going well. But the truth illustrated in Scripture is somewhat different. Psalm 23 is a good example. It is not that our lives will be full of success, with our heavenly Shepherd ensuring that we never walk through the valley of the shadow of death. Rather, the psalm suggests, we will all go there at one time or another, but when we are in such a valley, we will feel no fear. We will have the capacity to experience comfort. Our emotion and its bouquet of feelings, having been themselves transformed, will become even more deeply rooted in Christ rather than being buffeted and damaged by the superficial circumstances of our daily lives.

Many of us have tried to live this way in the past, but without the deep change that makes it possible. When fear, anxiety, or anguish begin to invade us, we practice a bit of "positive thinking." Encouraged by our cognitive upbringing, we try to gain the victory in Christ. But often what we are really doing, below the water line, is burying our anger. We believe that this is the Christian thing to do, that this is much more acceptable to the Lord. We assume that lots of anger cannot be good. It doesn't feel very Christlike. We recall those passages of Scripture that condemn such antisocial emotion and its behavior and convince ourselves that they give us permission to turn away and then deny the reality of what we really feel. If we practice such unhelpful behavior for long enough, we may almost be successful at convincing ourselves that such toxic and apparently unchristian feelings are really not there. But the tragedy is that by sublimating such feelings, to use the psychological term, we are also in danger of cutting one part of ourselves off from the other parts.

However, when we come together with others for any length of time, if we were simply to be spontaneous and real, such hidden emotion would very likely catapult itself into view. What if the person you most hate or despise happens to end up in your own small group? There is no way you could be "real" with them, is there? What if you've had a bad day with the boss (or a member of the congregation!) or had one of those PMT (premenstrual-tension) days? Surely no one is going to want to meet the person you really are? Meeting Jesus together becomes much more problematic.

The point is, of course, that if relationships are truly salugenic, then when we are more open and honest with others about these areas of emotion, we will allow them to lead us into more authentic Christlikeness. Instead of simply sharing a negative emotion, or repressing and denying it, we would find the resources within the group to use that moment in our lives to bring about deep and effective change. We all need to experience such deep emotional cleansing from our damaged historic emotion in order for us to begin enjoying more righteous and cleansed Christlike feelings.

In two of our forthcoming books we explore this tricky subject of emotion in far greater detail. One looks in a very practical way at how we can make greater use of our God-given gift of emotion and its feelings. The other looks at a biblical framework we can all adopt in order to become more like Christ emotionally, as recorded in Scripture.[1]

God clearly has deep emotions, and as we are made in His image, we should expect this area of our lives to need significant change as we grow in our journey toward greater Christlikeness. Likewise, when we become aware that Christ is present in our midst, one of the most common responses will be an emotional one, be it tears, joy, a feeling of shalom/peace, a new depth of love. All of these will bring greater wholeness to our emotion and its feelings. It is something we all need.

Our Behavior

Behavior is one of the more obvious areas in which change can be expected to take place when we know that Christ is present in our relationships with one another, or so many of us would say. The outer and more visible aspects of who we are can, we assume, be made to accommodate the expectations of Christlikeness. But with deep transformative change, nothing is quite that simple. We may be comfortably thinking that change in our behavior as we become more like Christ simply means that those unacceptable habits and addictions that we have will cease. We may also believe that we will become more polite and more loving. We will attend church and do a bit more to help others in some way. What we do not normally expect is that we will begin to breach some boundaries in our personal lives; for example, going to the desert to fast (or even the simple act of fasting). Perhaps we will end up breaking some religious conventions or offending those who seem to know God better than we do.

Some of Christ's behavior, as recorded in Scripture, was quite "outside the box"—eccentric, to say the least. It certainly broke the conventions and norms of the day, as well as offending His family and the religious leaders. His actions, whether staying asleep in the boat in the midst of the storm (Matthew 8:23–27), calling a group of uneducated and in some cases disreputable people to be His primary followers (for example, tax collectors, Matthew 10:3), or feeding four thousand men and their families from a small basket of bread and fish (Matthew 15:29–39), were not what would normally be thought of as best practice!

What about making mud pies out of one's spit and pushing it on eyes (John 9:6), His refusing to follow the rules of the Sabbath, or even chatting up a woman of questionable background? Are we ready to get this eccentric in our behavior as we become more Christlike? If we were to begin to behave in such eccentric ways, this would definitely make for some very unusual and different relationships!

One of the clearest areas of change as we grow in Christlikeness will be our ability to move in spiritual gifting. The exercise of our spiritual gifts, as we begin to find them, will have a profound impact on our behavior. For instance, when we exhibit wisdom, discernment, or knowledge, we will be able to respond in a completely different way to those around us. Likewise, when we find a specific ministry that we are really equipped for, our priorities will then need to change to accommodate it. In *Becoming More Like Christ* we identified a list of over thirty spiritual gifts and made the point that as we grow in Christlikeness our capacity to exercise them also increases significantly.[2] This will fundamentally impact every area of our behavior.

Of course, the most significant change in our behavior is that it becomes an expression of the change that is taking place at the core of our nature. When our spirit is overwhelmed with damage and/or when it is hidden, our behavior can be empty, shallow, and devoid of life. We "go through the motions" but cannot connect deeply with those sharing our actions because we have not connected deeply with ourselves. We are not present to ourselves, or to others, in our daily lives. Moreover, when Christ works to make His presence felt, our unwillingness to connect with the reality of our inner nature means that we inevitably resist Him. For He is most likely to be found in us in those places that we least want to go into ourselves. We would be among those in the crowd who stayed a safe distance rather than engaging with His words and deeds. Transformative change means a visibly different type of behavior as we discover the many things that Christ invites us to do that we are unaccustomed to doing and perhaps had not even wanted to think about.

Our Thinking

This third area of who we are is also one where we think we understand the need for change. Paul's exhortation "Be transformed by the renewing of your mind" (Romans 12:2) is a comfort to those of us who would like to focus more exclusively on our thinking as the most significant area of change. But should we perhaps be a little more cautious?

What is it that renews our minds? Can we use our thinking to change our thinking? It's a little like the conundrum of trying to pull yourself up by your own bootstraps. If you pull on the bootstraps of one foot, up comes your leg. If you pull on the bootstraps of the other foot, then up comes your other leg. But if you then want to lift yourself up by pulling on both bootstraps at the same time, you find it is simply not possible. The exercise of using our thinking to transform our thinking may achieve some modest change, but the renewal of our minds needs something much more radical.

In our ministry we talk about "God's perspective," His way of looking at a situation. When God interrupts our thinking with His perspective, those things we are "thinking" about are guaranteed to look radically different. He interrupts the obvious and will very likely put a completely different slant on what we thought we knew. Jesus gives a good example of such changed thinking in the Gospels. When He was teaching about those who went to see John the Baptist, He asked, "What did you go out into the desert to see?" (Luke 7:24). What did you think you would see? What we look for is what we find. Our expectations frequently (though not exclusively) contribute significantly to our subsequent experience.

So, what did people think about John the Baptist, as they sought him out in the desert? Was this merely a man in camel's hair clothes, eating locusts (Matthew 3:4)? Then perhaps that was all they found. If they had let their thinking be interrupted by God's perspective, however, their expectation would have been very different. John was the man who was preparing the way for the coming of the Son of God.

One of the driving forces of the life of a salugenic community is a hunger for God's perspective, so much so, that when God steps in and says, "Boo," there will very likely be a significant amount of change in all our lives. Developing the mind of Christ means discovering that our minds are the Enemy's playground (Romans 1:28; 8:6–7; Colossians 2:18; Titus 1:15, etc.). We are greatly in need of the transformative change that comes from God's perspective in order to undo the damage that has accrued in our minds.

Our Will

The final area of our personhood that we will mention as being deeply affected by the transformative change that Christ brings is our will. In fact, whether or not change is transformative and effective in our lives depends on our willed choices. Many of these choices can be quite deceptive.

We can behave in one way, while simultaneously resisting with our will. We go to school but do not want to learn. We go to church but do not want to worship. We say we want to diet but stubbornly keep eating all the wrong foods and refuse to exercise. This conflict or double standard in our behavior we often describe in our ministry as "hidden agendas." Transformative change happens when with every part of our being we are able to choose to change.

The will itself has to be changed along with other parts of who we are. Once again, this happens as we experience change in our spirits. The desires of our hearts are fundamentally affected by the healing and divine perspective that God brings. We are able to begin to want the things that God wants. This changes our wills and therefore has a huge impact on our capacity to change.

Having said that, we would add that much of the change in our lives is not consciously self-selected. Perhaps it has been imposed by others, or perhaps we commit to it to please others, rather than it being our own choice. We create the impression of preferring one set of choices, but these often conflict with those in our spirits that much of the time are below the water line of our conscious wills. In order for change to be effective, we must be able to embrace it personally and proactively, rather than passively and reluctantly.

We will return to the topic of choice in a later part of this book when we consider the importance Jesus placed on personal choice. What is interesting to note, however, is that transformative change will frequently mean an intentional exposing of our unhelpful hidden choices, followed by the subsequent changing of those choices.

Implications for Relationships

The suggestion we are making is that when we meet Jesus together, the change that results reaches into every part of who we are, every area of our lives. It is holistic. This means that our relationships need also to include a holistic dimension. They should include our emotion, our behavior, and our thinking, as well as exposing our will. Most of us have relationships that focus around areas of mutual interest. With other parents, we discuss schools, exam results, and the behavior of our children; with members of the sports team we discuss leagues, results, and injuries; while with work colleagues we talk about the trade or industry, the boss, and the (lack of) pay. Similarly, in church we talk about God, about our youth or mission programs, and about those other folk in the church we struggle with. Life can be about maintaining all these discrete and often private boxes.

How many of us belong to a small group where we each know one another so deeply that every area of who we are is included in our shared discussions? Even more demanding, will we, in those relationships, allow others to be the means of Christ bringing change across any or every part of our lives? To be known that fully can feel very frightening, even threatening.

We may have grown up enough in Christ to realize that we have no secrets from Him. We may even be aware that there are many things that we have not admitted to ourselves but that He is already fully aware of. When He is present as we meet in our twos and threes, He would very much like to bring that knowledge into the open. There should be no boundaries and barriers.

So if we continue to persist in having "no-go" areas in our relationships, we are putting obstacles in the path of our awareness of His presence. God is more eager to talk to us about what stands in His way in our lives than we are willing to let Him talk to us about what He sees. It is His perspective that matters, not ours.

We do have a caution. Letting others know everything about us gives them a lot of power in our lives. They are able to expose to us the hidden choices we are making that are obstructing the wholeness and Christlikeness that we claim to be seeking. And wherever there is power, there is a significant risk that it may be abused. Later in the book we will be showing how this is mediated to some degree in salugenic relationships because they are mutual by their very nature. This means that we each know everything about one another. The exposing of hidden choices happens with everyone. What we all have to learn, however, is that building and sustaining such relationships in a healthy, Christ-centered way takes time and must be done with significant care.

Our experience in our research and ministry has taught us that many people are in search of these holistic relationships where they can be more fully known. They bring loneliness to an end and offer security and the potential to build and develop greater self-esteem. The relationship is no longer task or activity based, but becomes person centered in a biblical, Christ-centered way, where the emphasis is not on self-esteem but on the quality and depth of the authenticity of the relationships. These relationships are of a similar type to those of the extended families and village-based communities that prevailed before industrialization and are still common in many non-Westernized parts of the world. Here, all your secrets are known by the community, and you likewise know all theirs. In the best communities there are a forgiving spirit and mutual support.

There is also, however, the potential for such communities to be discriminatory and judgmental. Fortunately, if salugenic relationships begin to become abusive, any member can choose either to challenge them openly or to withdraw. With practice, these relationships are able to remain Christ centered. When this happens, the experience of participating freely and mutually in such all-encompassing relationships can be life transforming.

One final comment needs to be made regarding emotion. The expression of emotion is often taboo in our relationships. But when any of us connect with our own deepest nature in our spirits, emotion will often come to the surface. Our experience is that salugenic groups will often draw to the surface the emotion that is in us that we simply do not know is there. Hurt, pain, betrayal, rejection, abandonment, anger, grief—all can surface and begin to manifest themselves, much to our surprise. Whatever the emotion, when salugenic relationships begin, the damaged emotion is never far away. However, in time, as you find deeper wholeness together, you will also find that it is God's feelings that begin to weigh more heavily. For as our emotion is cleansed and healed, we are more able to connect with how the Lord feels about matters in both our own lives and the lives of all those around us.

To Consider

- Which part of you will you find hardest to change? Why?
- What was your most recent experience of a change that affected several parts of your life?
- Think of a situation where you need God's perspective. Invite Him to step in and so radically transform your thinking and your hidden choices that significant change results. What in you might resist this change?

- Which emotion will be hardest for you to express in front of others? What needs to happen to help make you feel comfortable doing this?

CHAPTER 6

Relational Change

Our models of spiritual formation, especially in the Western evangelical church, have most frequently been people whose lives were private and personal, with very little shared. We seem to equate spiritual maturity with the strong, silent type, rather than the more open, spontaneous type of persona. Growth in Christlikeness is often expected to be an individualistic and restrained experience. Central to this is our emphasis on the personal quiet time where we meet privately with the Lord. Our faith is a personal relationship between us and God, and we rarely disclose it.

Christ's ministry, as we read about it in Scripture, often seems to be directly opposite to this private way of doing things. Change, when it occurred, was frequently public and involved engagement with others. For instance, most of the healings He performed were public events, as was much of His teaching. Even moments with some of the women, for example, the deliverance of Mary, were spoken about publicly. We should therefore expect the change Christ brings to us on our journeys to be no different.

Witnesses of the Change

In His ministry Jesus was unequivocal about the need to live our faith publicly. And one of the most dramatic changes that He expects others to see in us will be in our capacity to express love for one another: "By this all men will know that you are my disciples, if you love one another" (John 13:35). Although Scripture describes human nature as being full of darkness (Genesis 6:11–12; 8:21; Romans 3:9–18, etc.), Christ assumes that there will be a transformation in us, and one so extreme that others will notice. This suggests that the transformative change Christ brings will have a dramatic impact on our relationships and that the fruit of this change will be visible to those watching. It isn't even that we need to tell people we have changed. They will know, simply because the evidence will be unavoidable.

Have you ever met someone you knew well who had changed so significantly in a few days that it was immediately noticeable? We are not speaking here of a more stylish way of dressing or of a new dignity and assurance because of a new job, but a transformative change, one that seems in some inexplicable way to come from the inside out. Often the person is initially unaware of how much change has taken place and certainly would not expect others to notice. You can't quite put your finger on what is different, but your relationship is immediately affected. You feel that you want to respond differently, but you are not sure how to. In some strange way, the change seems to require a change in you.

Here is where such positive change becomes relational and contagious. It is impossible for us to stay the same if we are in close relationships with others who are experiencing transformative change. Our thinking, values, agendas, and attitudes are all challenged. Our oneness is also affected. Part of the body has grown, and we all have the opportunity to benefit.

When I (Susan) was going through a particularly intense time of personal change,[1] I had a strange pattern of experiences that took me some time to understand. I would go to church on a Sunday, and several people would mention at some time during the meeting that they loved my new outfit and that it really suited me. I would thank them, appreciative of the compliment, albeit a little self-conscious. However, I would go away puzzled. This was not a new outfit, but something I had worn a number of times before. It was several months before I noticed that these remarks would always occur at the end of a week where I had had a specific experience of some form of change, usually a deep cleansing of damage I had been carrying for years. They were feeling the change in my spirit but couldn't account for it, so instinctively assumed it was my clothes.

Transformative change is like this—even without our words, others will feel the difference. But the relational element of this change is not simply that others notice. They themselves, sometimes kicking and screaming, are also drawn into the slipstream.

Creating a "Holy Synergy"

It was one of the most remarkable things that happened when we planted Christ Church Deal, yet it was some time before we noticed the miracle that was taking place before our eyes. We had lots of people who were experiencing transformative change, and they were talking about it together. Most weeks in our Sunday service someone would give a testimony about a recent experience of increased wholeness or a deeper encounter with Christ. They would speak publicly and quite specifically about the damage and sin that had been in their life and how God had stepped in to bring them healing. Others would share their experience in small groups.

These stories would then become the talking point of the community. When God had stepped in with one person, they would then offer to support another who might want to experience a similar area of healing. This would create seasons of change. Perhaps one month God would move through the congregation, bringing healing from grief and loss. Then another month He would show many how to let go of their anger. This might be followed by a period of time in which a number were restored in their relationship with the Lord.

We suddenly realized that a holy synergy was occurring. The anointing from one "miracle" was unleashing a whole series of related miracles. They were just as supernatural but would often follow a similar pattern. It was as if God could get more miles to the gallon from everything that we were doing because we were sharing it with others! One word, one moment of intervention in the life of a member of the church, would produce change in many others.

This is a dynamic that we also see in Scripture. The transformation of the woman at the well led many others to believe in Christ (John 4:39). She was generous with the news about what was happening in her life, even though the conversation had exposed more than she was comfortable with. Because of her conversations and declarations, others were able to experience similar change. When Christ is in our midst and when we are real with one another, transformative change can spread like wildfire. It is the tinder of Christ's anointing in our midst, and the Holy Spirit lights it with love.

Changing with One Another

There are lots of things about all of us that make us quite difficult to love. Even the most mature of us have our little (and not-so-little) quirks and foibles that grate against those who come near us. Of course, we often have more serious areas of sin or parts of our lives where we struggle to walk in obedience to Christ. There are also those areas where we have been hurt by others or by circumstances. Such areas can often leave lingering damage that has perhaps not yet been fully healed.

What one learns over time on this kind of change journey is that we will often have to go through several layers before we expose the core issue or problem. Getting to the right layer or the right question can be much of the battle. Each of these parts of our nature will present a challenge when we are living in relationship with others. If we were alone, we would perhaps find ways of minimizing the impact of who we have become, but others seem to have the ability to draw it to the surface. Our need to change increases significantly when we commit to meeting Jesus together

When we love another, we want to change for their sake. For instance, we want to minimize the risk of hurting them. In fact, we will do whatever is necessary to preserve and develop the relationship. So living a life of love for those around us means we will continually be needing to change. The simple command of Christ was that we love one another. Such love was not an option, nor was it restricted to those we found easy to love. Everyone can love their friends and even most of their family, but we are also called to love our "enemies" (Luke 6:27). Christ did not ask us simply to be nice to them or to tell them "have a good day"! He did not even stop at asking us to bless them. Quite unambiguously, we are called to love them. This type of love requires that we change, for none of us naturally loves those who do not love us. And this type of change requires the removal of all the baggage that stands in the way of our being unwilling to love those who hate us and that hinders our capacity to love. Because we have to learn to love those who we would perhaps instinctively back off from. By doing so God's love is made complete in us (1 John 2:5).

Scripture is clear, therefore, that our discipleship journey should directly involve relationships with others. Such relationships should be a means of our being able to "spur one another on" (Hebrews 10:24). One of my (Susan's) favorite images in Scripture is of the moment when Jesus invited those around Lazarus to take off his grave-clothes. Of course, Christ could have given a command, and in an instant those grave-clothes would have fallen off. But Christ had a greater goal in mind—that the whole community should participate in Lazarus's coming back to life (John 11:17–44). For Lazarus, even here the change was relational.

Implications for Relationships

It might appear a tautology to say that the relational aspects of transformative change have implications for our relationships. But it is an important point. In order to change we need one another's help. Relationships that recognize this goal in our lives and in the lives of others can become significant, lifelong friendships. This means, however, that one of the goals and focal points of the relationships is the encouragement of growth, personal development, and any form of positive change. Such change becomes the common denominator in our relationships. This is in some ways very uncomfortable, as well as being counterintuitive. It is usual to build relationships around what can stay the same, what we have in common; but salugenic relationships, by contrast, are in constant change. In these relationships, the one thing you can be most certain of is that in a few weeks' time there will be a significant difference. Over time such relationships become the focus of our lives, the norm, and the high points of our lives.

When you get used to this aspect of a small group that is meeting Jesus together, you find it very liberating. For as long as all the members of the group want to carry on exploring their journeys of becoming more of the people they were created to be, the relationships have purpose and urgency. There is a shared commitment and a common focus. These are relationships that are focused on the needs of the other people. What change is best for them? What change are they seeking? The change in their lives might not be what suits us best. It might, for example, mean they have less time for us for a season. But this is offset by the fact that they are also treating us in the same way. We have allowed them to know the areas of change that we are seeking; and they, in their turn, are willing to make these a priority. Instead of each person tacitly protecting their own interests, there is an openly discussed agenda of each person supporting radical, ongoing growth in another's life. This is a radically different type of friendship. It is, we would suggest, a fundamental part of the love by which others will know that we are disciples of Christ.

To Consider

- Which would you prefer, change that is private or change that is relational? Why?
- How would you choose others to help you change?
- What qualities would you look for in another who would be making the journey of change with you?
- What support are you able to offer to help a friend on their journey toward greater Christlikeness?

CHAPTER 7

In Summary

In this second part of our exploration of salugenic community we have considered what type of change might be precipitated when we are aware of Christ's presence among us. What type of change happens when we meet Jesus together?

We have seen that, first, it occurs deep in the core of our beings, but, second, it also impacts every area of our lives, bringing an end to the fragmentation and the boxes that we have been accustomed to for so long. As a result, instead of being divided, with the different parts of ourselves in conflict, the result is an unimaginably deep oneness.

Transformative change goes further than this, however. The third aspect of this change is that it challenges our perception of ourselves as independent individuals. It is when we are together with others in Christ's name that we most enjoy the richness of His presence. These relationships are integral to our journey into wholeness. It is the reality of our being "together" that enables us to meet Jesus in a deeper way.

But there are two other characteristics of transformative change that we must now move on to if we are to ensure that we are more effectively equipped to build relationships that will enable this miraculous journeying.

Part 3
DYNAMICS AND DIRECTION

Transformative change is a journey that has a clear direction and purpose. It brings increasing Christlikeness to all who share in it and increases our capacity to meet Jesus together. But this is not simply a gradual change. It is a journey interrupted by many moments so significant that they are often recognized as miraculous. Building relationships that have such a clear focus and ongoing change is not easy.

"CHANGE" IS A POPULAR WORD IN OUR CULTURE, AND CERTAINLY THE world we live in is full of change. American presidential candidates, whichever party they belong to, use it as one of their buzzwords. International insurance companies claim it makes the need for their protection greater than ever. The climate is changing; technology is changing; even the pace of change is changing.

Today we experience change in numerous ways, some nice, others decidedly nasty. We welcome change in our job, if it means promotion or a higher salary, but struggle when that change is forced on us, or we are required to learn a new skill or get a different qualification. Some change is spontaneous, some more gradual. Sometimes we adjust, while other types of change we resist throughout our lives and only submit when we have no other choice.

The type of change we are talking about on this journey is quite specific. Let us add two more aspects of it to our growing understanding.

CHAPTER 8

Discontinuous Change

We move now to the fourth characteristic of the type of change that should be normal in our lives as we grow in Christlike wholeness. It focuses on the form or nature of change.

Much of the change in our lives, both inside and outside the church, occurs gradually. Developmental psychology and Erikson's stage development theory both map the gradual progression of the typical psychological growth of the individual.[1]

Much writing on spiritual formation will refer to the maturity that accrues through the daily practice of the spiritual disciplines. Such change is an essential part of our ongoing discipleship journey.

Transformative change, however, has a different emphasis. It focuses on those moments when something that was is now gone, and something new is birthed. It is not based simply on a continual or gradual progression of change. Instead, it is the result of something that is interrupted. There is a moment when the continuity is broken. What was there is there no longer, and something different is going on. We are describing a highly visible change from one thing to another. In Jesus' life, the clearest examples are, of course, the miracles He performed.

The Miraculous

Being around Christ was exciting. Change was going on everywhere all the time in different people. It was highly visible and quite remarkable.

Jesus seemed to break the rules of what was possible. Those who had been lame all their lives were able to begin dancing. Those who had lived isolated existences in caves, chained up for their own safety and that of others, were able to live among family and friends and testify to their healing and growing wholeness.

There were examples of more gradual change, too. Much of the disciples' own journeys was a result of being around Him, listening, learning, and growing. But it was the change that was more spectacular that was more noticeable.

It would be easy for us to say that Christ was the only one for whom this discontinuous change was the norm. But Scripture does not allow us to come to that conclusion. Look at the life of the early church in Acts or Christ's simple promise that we would do greater things than He had done so far (John 5:20; 14:12). And when He speaks of our authority to bind and loose as part of the Great Commission (Matthew 16:18–19; 18:18; 28:16–20), He is certainly suggesting something discontinuous!

The most obvious time in our Christian lives when discontinuous change is known is at conversion. For many this moment of being born again, a change from darkness to light, is a significant experience of transformative change. Others experience something similar in their encounters with the Holy Spirit. But our contention in this book is that these moments of discontinuous change should continue in two ways throughout our journey into greater Christlikeness.

First, the change should continue in our own lives. None of us is without sin, and we cannot expect to be without sin this side of death (Romans 3:23). However, we can expect that the power of sin will be broken and that we will know God's forgiveness. It would be great if this were a once-for-all experience, but the reality is very different. Overcoming the power of this damage is something we do one area at a time, one after another.

Paul made it clear in Romans that his battle to become more Christlike was an ongoing journey (Romans 7:15–20; 8:6–7). Suppose you have identified five areas where your experience is similar to Paul's. In these areas you simply keep finding that you do not do the good you want to do. But on your journey of transformative change, you will find that each pattern will be undone, one at a time, and you will be changed as a result. God will want to go deeper in your life and show you more areas, but the ones you tackle are transformed into areas of wholeness in your life.

Perhaps one of the five areas you have identified is your failure to love someone. One day the pattern of despising that person is still in place; the next it is gone. Perhaps it is an area of skill in your career. On one day you cannot make a presentation while using PowerPoint effectively; the next you can. That is a discontinuous type of change. Throughout our lives, if we continue growing in our Christlikeness, there will be ongoing discontinuous change in a variety of areas.

The second way in which we experience ongoing discontinuous change should be in the lives of those around us. It is Christ's norm that we should participate in helping to achieve this change in the lives of others in our churches and small groups. When they change, we are changed because we are one with them. We can celebrate the radical transformation they have experienced. Instead of applauding from the sidelines or, worse, perhaps even judging the change they are claiming, we become part of their experience of discontinuous change. This is what happens when we meet Jesus together.

Tipping Points

In the 1990s Malcolm Gladwell popularized the concept of "tipping points."[2] These are the moments when one little step forward produces a consequence of disproportionate significance. He gives an example from marketing: One day a brand of trainers is hardly known, and then, after simply one more advert in a run of twenty, there is an unquenchable demand. Or if we were to look at a flu epidemic, we find that one day just one more person falls ill, but two days later schools and workplaces are emptied as a huge number of people are affected. It seems that the discontinuous change of tipping points is expressed in nature, in the social world, and in our personal lives.

Think of children learning to read. They begin by learning one-syllable words but then go on to learn more complex words. There is a gradual change from one week to the next. But normally at some point these changes will accumulate so significantly that it will be clear that they can now read. At the beginning of the year, they couldn't, but now they can. They have crossed a threshold, a tipping point.

The same is true of someone learning to swim or learning to ride a bicycle. There is a particular threshold that is crossed. Before it the learner could not swim and would fall off a bicycle. After their tipping point they can swim without flotation support, and they can ride without stabilizers. Rather than being one little step forward, they have a new skill. Having a baby is another, rather visible, tipping point. The woman might spend many hours in labor, and during this time she is very specifically "having the baby." Nonetheless, there is a moment when the baby was not visible and another moment when the baby is born.

Transformative change is like this in our lives. We might spend a period of time wanting to let go of our anger toward someone. Again and again we might reassert our choice to forgive them. But the tipping point is when we know, from the very core of our being, that the anger is gone. Likewise, we might know in our understanding that God loves us; we might even declare it in faith many times over. But when we have experienced it incontrovertibly, we are changed forever. We have experienced that tipping point. God loves me.

In some ways, to expect only gradual change may be all too easy a way of letting ourselves off the hook. If there is no expectation of a visible, palpable change, then neither we nor others can say that it has or has not happened. We are less accountable and less responsible. It leads to the kind of question that we both (Peter and Susan) get asked in our workshops and seminars—how will I know when I'm healed? The answer is very simple—when the damage is not there any longer!

There is, of course, a danger of polarizing things too much. Not all areas in our lives have significant boundaries marked by discontinuous change. Intimacy with Christ, for example, is a gradual journey that we will all be on for the rest of our lives. But as authors we would expect that if you were to focus on the small steps that make up that journey, you would find many visible tipping points.

In *Becoming More Like Christ* we included a meditation to help the reader meet Jesus in a specific "room" of their spiritual house and work with Him to clean up the room and restore it to the way God intended it to be.[3] Such a journey involves many tipping points. Perhaps there is a specific corner of that room where there has been a lot of pain, or perhaps the demeaning words of others have been ricocheting from wall to wall. But then a threshold is crossed, Christ brings healing to those areas of damage, and the room feels noticeably different. Perhaps later there is a bigger tipping point when we feel that the whole room has been cleaned out and redecorated with the Lord and now carries the anointing of His presence instead of the barrenness of our own personal history.

Implications for Relationships

In salugenic relationships there is the expectation that discontinuous change will, over time, be experienced by every member of the group. Each of us will know our own miracles, created by the presence of Christ in our midst but supported by others on the journey with us. After a while the group becomes a safe place in which to share these experiences and to affirm the visible change in one another's lives. Those who feel themselves on the verge of that change can openly share their hopes and fears. Each person should participate in the drama of the tipping point of another, knowing that this type of change should be normal and that soon it will be their turn.

Discontinuous change has its downside, of course. It can be quite disruptive to day-to-day relationships. While undergoing such change, it is easy to slip into inconsistent or less-than-ideal behavior. Perhaps we prove to be unreliable, or we get angry or are absentminded. We might lose interest in a shared hobby or feel that we have no energy to engage in conversation. For those observing such change in us, the relationships may temporarily no longer feel quite so mutual, their needs may not be met, or the aspect of the relationship they valued the most might slip off our priority list. Tipping points can be quite antisocial.

However, it is in the midst of this type of change that we most need the consistency of deep friendships with others who will tolerate our behavior and forgive us for our frailty. Also, they will continue to believe in the change that they likewise are pursuing. It is too easy to lose perspective or feel overwhelmed by the magnitude of what Christ is doing in the lives of all those in the group. It is very important that these difficulties should be openly discussed. If they are part of the group's shared experience, and if they are considered part of the norm of the journey of ongoing Christlikeness, the community will undoubtedly find ways of overcoming those more challenging moments. And they then pale into insignificance once the transformative change becomes visible and is witnessed to by the rest of the group.

To Consider

- What would be uncomfortable about discontinuous change in your church or small group?
- What could you do to be more supportive and to make it easier for such change to take place?
- What is your most recent example of discontinuous change?

CHAPTER 9

Choosing Christlikeness

Our final characteristic of transformative change is that it is specifically change that leads to increased wholeness and Christlikeness. Meeting Jesus leads to more of Jesus.

Our life is full of change. Each change has the capacity to influence us in a different way. Some changes create opportunities, others feel as if they confine or limit us. Some changes bring hope, while other forms of change can lead to despair. The type of transformative change that God intends to be the norm for us all is change that enables our growth.

Becoming Who You Were Created to Be

Transformative change is all about the potential we each have to become the person we were created to be. Imagine if there had been no mistakes, no suffering, no unpleasant circumstances or relationships in our pasts. Let us imagine someone who had had the world's most supportive and stimulating upbringing, surrounded by others who were successfully introducing them to Father, Son, and Holy Spirit and to their journey of becoming the person they were created to be. Imagine that they had made the wisest choices and consistently taken every opportunity to grow. There is a good chance that they would at, say, the age of thirty-five, be close to the potential of who God had created them to be.

Sadly, this is not the case with most of us. We all live in a fallen world and have been the victims of damage from a wide variety of sources, including our own unwise decisions and actions. We have become very different from the people we were created to be. For many of us, the size of the gap is unbearable. Were we to look at ourselves from God's perspective, the gap between who we now are and who we should be would be even larger.

It is always a challenge to spend some time considering who we would have had the potential of being. One of the images I (Susan) sometimes used in my workshops was of a lone unicorn standing on the shore and looking out at Noah's ark as it sailed away into the distance. It is fictitious, of course! Yet it makes the point that many of us feel that the potential of who we really could have been has gone forever. Scripture, however, affirms the opposite of such despair. God is Redeemer. He works redemption in our lives by taking that which is damaged, sick, and apparently beyond repair and then beginning to restore it. We have written elsewhere about the principle of Jehovah Rapha.[1] Our favorite paraphrase is "I am the mender, the one who sews you together, into Christ" (Exodus 15:26).

Transformative change is a change that takes the reality of who we have become and, layer by layer, room by room, brings about more of the reality of who we were created to be. It is not that the person we were created to be is gone forever. Rather, it is that our awareness and capacity to live as that person have been swamped by the day-to-day reality of living in this world. A room may be magnificently decorated, but you would never know it if you couldn't get in the door because of the clutter.

There is excellence in all of us. Everything that God has created is "good"—a biblical understatement! The transformative change that God wants to bring is to let that goodness shine through, to let it be restored to us. But that means that we have to first believe that such a journey might be possible, both for us and for others; and then we have to learn how to walk it. When we see it begin to happen in the lives of those around us, we are given more courage to raise the expectation of our own redemption, too.

Let us give you some examples. Think of a man who has served the Lord "full time" most of his adult life. On this journey he discovers a gift he has of botanical art that allows him to win medals at international horticultural exhibitions. Or an audiovisual technician who finds he can do a PhD in international law. Imagine a mental health worker who becomes a fully qualified probation officer, or a transport manager who becomes a foster parent for children from difficult backgrounds. Think of a mother with little education who does a degree in theology and also discovers she is a prophetess or of a pharmacist who has to admit he has an anointing for preaching while also following up his ambition of becoming a commercial pilot. We could give you hundreds more illustrations and introduce you to the people and the journeys that led to the redemption they experienced. All of us have the potential of becoming more of the people we were created to be.

Wholeness and Christlikeness

In *Becoming More Like Christ* we drew together three distinct terms related to the idea of spiritual formation: Christian maturity, wholeness, and Christlikeness. We suggested that these concepts are intertwined. They may come from slightly different traditions and have different writings associated with them, but our experience is that, from God's perspective, they are each a different slant on the one same truth—the potential that we all have of becoming the people we are created to be.

This suggestion is fundamental to salugenic relationships and to meeting Jesus together. It creates the foundation for the oneness that we share together in Christ. The person we were created to be is, of course, Christlike. But although we are all made in the image of God, none of us was born Christlike, or becomes Christlike merely by wishing it. Likewise, we are all, even in this damaged world, designed to become more whole than we already are. For the God-breathed resilience in our spirits and the capacities of our bodies enable us both to retain holiness and to continue growing in even deeper wholeness, despite all the sufferings and setbacks of life.

Christ is our true and authentic definition of wholeness. He was fully God, carrying the full image and glory of God, while also being fully human. Adam and Eve gave away the dignity of humanity when they turned away from God and began to make choices independent of Him. By doing so, they became less than the people God created them to be. In tasting the fruit of "the tree of the knowledge of good and evil," they gained the knowledge of choice that God had not given them. In separating themselves from God, in taking on that which was not from God, they lost their wholeness with God. We have been living ever since in the slipstream of those choices and their earth-shattering tragedy.

It is amazing, is it not, that Christ offers us an escape from this tragedy? Rather than simply condemning us to live with the fragments of damaged humanity that we were left with, He offers us wholeness. Rather than leaving us to live in the shadow land of what we now understand as being human, He brings us the humanness He had intended. Christ is our example of this way of life. He offers us the opportunity of "becoming more human," for what He created He also called "good."

Wholeness and Christlikeness are, from God's perspective, the same. Christ is the example of who we should become. Both wholeness and Christlikeness are a redemption of the dignity of divinity in humanity that God intended all of us to enjoy. The full abundance of who we were created to be will be possible only when we are fully restored to Christ. But far more is available to us in this life than any of us would dare to imagine.

Creating More Becoming

There is the slight risk, as we consider this journey, that we will slip into a mindset that thinks that God has already dictated who we should be and that our responsibility is to learn about that person and then do our best to fit into that mold. Nothing could be further from the truth.

There is little in Scripture that suggests that God has laid down tramlines that we should walk in order to please Him. We do not have a God who monitors our every step to see if it is exactly as He ordained it. Instead, God looks toward our hearts or our spirits, the core of who we are. He focuses on why we do what we do (Matthew 12:34; Lk 6:45), on what drives or motivates us. For instance, it is not a question of how you use your time, but of what motivates you in your use of your time.

Scripture is clear that God delights to give the "desires of your heart" (Psalm 37:4). This requires that we take responsibility for finding those desires and then playing our part in making them a reality. Many of us have had those desires squashed over the years. Our wholeness means having the courage to begin to find them again.

God wrote the template of who we could become; we were His idea; He knows us. This person may be deeply buried and to begin with may not even be recognizable to us. But God will restore all that He intended for us and for us to become if we are willing to welcome this person to us.

The Christlike wholeness that God wants to restore to us is an ongoing act of creation in our lives. In this sense, Christ is the agent of our journey of recovery, for His presence inspires it, as His love motivates it. While He was on earth, He achieved change in the lives of those who came to Him, and in the same supernatural way He wants to bring about change for us today in the twenty-first century.

But in that process of change Christ does not act unilaterally. Even when the Israelites got their first glimpse of freedom after slavery, Jehovah Rapha made it clear that partnership was the order of the day: "If you listen carefully to the voice of the LORD your God and do what is right in his eyes, if you pay attention to his commands . . ." (Exodus 15:26). The Israelites had their part to play to enable God to fulfill His promise in their lives. It is much easier for us to sit praying that God will bring to us the wholeness that He desires. We can be heartfelt in our prayer that God will make us into the people He has created us to be. And this is certainly a good start. But that act of redemption is far more of a partnership than we are often comfortable with. Our wrong choices and our ill-informed priorities can be insurmountable obstacles to our own prayer. Alternatively, our prayers can create a momentum that God can then steer and direct.

Christ expects us to do for one another what He did in the lives of the early disciples, though achieving even greater things (John 14:12). As we journey together with Him, so we will achieve the creation of greater Christlikeness in our own lives and in each other's lives.

Implications for Relationships

Our wholeness is much bigger, much richer, much deeper than we dare to believe. It has the potential of Christ Himself in it. But it can never be achieved in isolation. Wholeness that is independent of either Christ or others is, from God's perspective, an oxymoron. If we want to grow in Christlike wholeness, we have to accept that, according to the way we are designed, wholeness is relational. Becoming the people we are created to be also means growing more deeply in relationships with others.

It is an awesome privilege to be part of the growing wholeness of others and to share with them in their growing Christlikeness. Not only do we have the pleasure of seeing others grow more into the people they were created to be, but as they grow, so do we, and then as we grow, so do they.

The challenge for such relationships is that we are very likely to become different as we become more of ourselves in Christ. Later in the book we will refer to this as "uniqueness." Although we are all created to become more like Christ, this does not mean conformity to a stereotype of a godly woman or man. The more like Christ we become, the more unique we become.

Much of our identity is defined by our difference from other people, rather than our similarity. Key stages in a child's development are achieved when the child is able to distinguish between himself or herself and another. Part of a healthy process of growing up is the parent's acknowledgment of the uniqueness of the child. Likewise, teenage years are characterized by young adults identifying ways in which they are going to be independent of their parents. In just the same way, our relationships have to be such that we can encourage growth that makes someone different from us, without our fearing the consequences for ourselves.

To Consider

- What aspect of your wholeness do you want to focus on? How can you begin this process?
- What area of your life do you feel is least Christlike? How has it come to be this way?
- Who are the people who are participating in the creation of Christlikeness in your life?
- Who are the people who have invited you to participate in the creation of Christlikeness in their lives? What can you do to make their journey more effective?

CHAPTER 10

In Summary

We have been looking at the idea that change is at the heart of the gospel and is an essential part of the message of Christ. It has to be this way; otherwise, how will we change to become more mature in Christ and able to "grow up" in the Lord? The way we have described it, this journey includes moments of marked and noticeable change, discontinuous with what went before. It is, of course, salugenic in nature—it creates wholeness. Moments when we know we have met together in Christ's presence are moments that build the dynamic for transformative change.

There are times on our discipleship journey when it is particularly easy to see how the outworking of this salugenic type of change applies. Conversion is the most obvious example. Though many begin their relationship with God without experiencing significant change, it is clear from Scripture that the move "from darkness into light" is one that we should expect to happen and also expect to make a noticeable difference in our lives. Likewise, those who know they are in need will find significant change when their need is met.

The situation is slightly different for those of us who are more experienced in Christ and without any pressing need that we have identified. Perhaps we do not feel a particular need to change. Should transformative personal change still apply to us? Our own experience tells us that the answer to this question is a resounding "yes." We are proposing that this journey of transformative change need never stop. Even as our most immediate need is healed, the journey of change continues. Perhaps our journey of becoming who we were created to be will involve us in stretching ourselves professionally, growing in our capacity as a parent, or playing our part in our local community. For some of us it might mean change toward an increase in our capacity to exercise spiritual gifting or in our ability to disciple others.

Whatever the area of growth and change that is needed in our lives, we are proposing that it should involve transformative change. Because of Christ, we all have the potential to see miraculous change in our lives and in the lives of others. These are levels of change, that is, that would not be possible without the presence of Christ. We all carry damage from our history that God wants to undo so that we may be released into more of the people we were created to be.

You will have noticed that we have not talked in any detail about how that change is achieved. That is not the focus of this book. We have, however, included several practical suggestions in the penultimate chapter. In *Becoming More Like Christ* we included a chapter with specific suggestions on how you might want to begin your own journey, and in *Changed Lives* a number of others describe how this journey has successfully worked in their lives, with background explanation from us. We have numerous other materials that help describe in some detail how the change can happen.[1]

Salugenic relationships are primarily relationships that support and enable the journey of change that each of us chooses to commit to. The presence of Christ and relationships with others on the journey propel us into deeper, more determined, and more effective levels of change. Having people we can call on, people who understand, who are doing the same journey themselves, also allows us to let the Lord take us to new areas of redemption and transformation in our own lives. Together we discover more wholeness and more of Christ.

The next questions that we need to address are: What type of environment and what type of relationships can help release and sustain this transformative change? What does this salugenic faith community really look like? And if this is what happens when we are aware that Christ is in our midst, what can we do to ensure that there is nothing in our relationships with one another that will hinder these processes? Or, to put that in a more proactive context: What can we do to build relationships that enable the transformative change that Christ wants to bring? How can we more effectively support the process of meeting Jesus together?

Part 4
QUALITIES OF SALUGENIC RELATIONSHIPS

It is not easy to build relationships that allow us to consistently meet Jesus together. It is a hard fact that salugenic community does not come naturally to any of us. But if we understand some of its most important qualities, there is a lot we can each do to play our part in creating the relationships that make this more likely.

IN AN IDEAL WORLD, EVERY BELIEVER WOULD BE ENJOYING THE experience of the palpable presence of Christ together with others. Soon after beginning their relationship with God, all believers would know what it is to take their places within the body of Christ, learning to be one with other members of this body. They would become intimately familiar with the significance of Christ's promise that He is present where two or three are gathered in His name. They would also have a growing hunger for these remarkable salugenic communities and would be developing skill in creating and living in them.

Sadly, we don't live in an ideal world. For many of us, our church experience has been at best inconsistent. There may have been times when we were part of groups that experienced the reality of the presence of Christ. But it is likely that we have known many groups that were more barren and even cold and uninviting.

For others of us church life has become a merry-go-round of teaching and activity. A Sunday is judged a success if the preacher was on form and the youth program went well. There are often as many people in church we would rather avoid as there are folk we would want to be one with. We may be bored with it all and feel we have still not found what we are looking for. The whole experience of church is a very mixed blessing!

Many of us can cite some occasional relationships that have been salugenic. They may have been brief encounters with a person or a group that suddenly unleashed a wave of personal growth or change in us or in others. Or perhaps they were a group of friendships that extended over time in which we witnessed or experienced significant change. They may have happened in church, but maybe not. Some Christians have even concluded that some of their most salugenic relationships have occurred with those who apparently had no faith. How does that work? We will comment later.

If one of our goals is to have Christ-centered relationships that achieve oneness and promote meeting Jesus together, where do we start? If we want to be part of a salugenic community that is successfully pursuing transformative change and becoming more Christlike, what will it really look like?

In this part of the book we will look at three characteristics that are integral to salugenic communities. Each is simple enough to be the basis of guidelines that can then be practiced together in a very clear and direct way. We have again included some questions at the end of each section for you to consider, if you are finding that helpful. We have also added questions for you to discuss together with a group of others on the same mission.

CHAPTER 11

Acceptance

Everywhere Jesus went He offered people acceptance. Some came with the awareness of their sin, for example, the woman caught in adultery (John 8:3–11) or Peter when Jesus called him back to Himself (John 21:15–22). Others came and found their sin exposed, for example, the woman at the well (John 4:1–26) or the rich ruler who thought he kept all the commandments but discovered he worshiped money (Luke 18:18–23). Some were social outcasts (Luke 19:1–10); others were members of the ruling party (John 3:1–13). Some asked for help (Mark 7:26), and others, such as the demon-possessed man, received help before they asked (Luke 8:26–39). All were offered acceptance by the King of Kings.

All of us need people who will accept us unconditionally. It's what a baby should experience from its parents. William James, a founder of modern psychology, highlighted the craving to be appreciated as a fundamental drive in human nature.[1] That craving is especially heightened when we are at our most vulnerable. When we have our defenses up, we may pretend the craving is not there, but the truth is that at the very core of our beings, if we are to live in Christlike wholeness, we all need to know that we are loved, that we are accepted. We need to know that we have found a home in God.

In my (Susan's) research, the experience of being accepted was a fundamental precursor to salugenic relationships and therefore salugenic community. To allow ourselves to experience oneness, we have to know that we are accepted as we are and also be willing to offer the same acceptance to others.[2]

The outcome of salugenic relationships is that we will move on, that we will grow and change to become more like Christ. It is somewhat paradoxical, therefore, that one of the things that helps us move on in this way is being in relationships where we know that such change is not required! We need to know that we are deeply and unconditionally accepted, that we are loved and valued, just the way we are!

When we have experienced such acceptance and have begun to trust it, we are then able to choose for ourselves whether and when we want to begin to change. This is not change and growth in order to survive or change that is imposed by others. Instead, it is change that we select as part of our ongoing growth and development. Acceptance produces far more effective long-term change than overt or subtle manipulation! We are loved by the Beloved One.

Acceptance is one of those words that is easy to say, yet much harder to pin down. So in order to create relationships based on acceptance we have to be more specific. We have identified three different facets of acceptance that combine to help lay the foundation for salugenic relationships.

Personal Worth

For Christians, at the heart of acceptance, is the acknowledgment that every human being is created by God and that He called everything He created "good." There is no doubt that every part of who we are has been contaminated by "a disease called sin,"[3] but we are, nonetheless, "fearfully and wonderfully made" (Psalm 139:14). It is this emphasis on our value to our Creator that undergirds acceptance. He thought that we were a good idea and loves us.

This principle of personal self-worth has radical implications for the body of Christ. We see again and again in Scripture that Christ commands us to love. This love extends to small children, to strangers, and even to our enemies. We are to treat one another as if we have personal worth, knowing that we are indeed recognized and treasured in the sight of God (1 Corinthians 12:1–26). You have perhaps heard the phrase "love the sinner but hate the sin." The recognition of personal worth acknowledges that however much damage we have in our lives, however many mistakes, or however severe our antisocial habits, we are loved by God.

Love does not mean condoning sin. We have seen that in Christ's life. His form of love results in sin being exposed (see chapter 11). But even when this occurred, the person always knew that they were being treated as a person of worth, for it is the loving father who disciplines his children (Hebrews 12:5–11). Our Creator loves us, in loving what He has created. Personal worth means embracing the sinner, rather than the sin.

When we practice the principle of personal worth in our relationships, it means that our starting point is our awareness that the other person and we ourselves are important to God. When we meet a visitor or a new member to our community, even before we know anything about them, we can treat them as someone who has worth and significance. Our leaders, and those who have failed most publicly, should be equally valued, especially for who they were created to be in Christ. This may all sound simple, but it is in fact a challenging way to live.

Personal Uniqueness

There is an additional dimension to acceptance that often represents even more of a challenge, especially in our church life. If we are to accept the worth of the other person, we will inevitably have to value the fact that they are different from us. Every single one of us on the face of the earth is unique in every way, be it in our DNA, our saliva, our fingerprints, our eye design, our voice, or even our knowledge. No one else is even close to being like us. God has made every one of us unique.

Living with the knowledge of that uniqueness can be a challenge. Though at first this might sound simple, on a daily basis it can be quite demanding, for several reasons. First, relationships work most easily when we have a lot in common. It is what we share together that creates the foundation for relationship. So there is a natural tendency to minimize our differences for the sake of building relationships. Yet we are suggesting that in Christ, valuing our differences is a fundamental part of body life (1 Corinthians 12:12–19). We would even go further and suggest that local churches need to learn to celebrate their diversity and uniqueness.

Uniqueness also brings a challenge to the dynamic of role models. Many of us have lived with an understanding (perhaps unspoken) that Mrs. A is an example of a godly woman, that Mr. B the epitome of fatherhood, while Mr. C an exemplar of a worship leader. Growing in Christ, we have assumed, means learning from these role models to increase our own maturity. Instead, we are suggesting that our only role model is Christ, whom we will become like as we welcome the uniqueness of the people He created us to be.

So we are proposing something that has a radically different dynamic from the one we are accustomed to. When uniqueness is valued in our relationships, we will each assume that the other's growth will be quite different from our own. When we see a difference, therefore, we will not seek to increase conformity. We will avoid the temptation of trying to make them more like we think they should be, that is, more like us. Instead, we will help the person explore their own unique differences and treasure these, while perhaps having to clean them up from some of their more unholy tendencies.

Uniqueness prioritizes our eccentricities, the unusual and the remarkable. So as we grow in Christ on this journey, we become more unique while also becoming more like everyone else by becoming more like Christ. Living this way means that the individuality of each person is more fully recognized by them and others. Variety and its subsequent diversity become more important than conformity.

Discipleship journeys also become more unique as each person's own need and potential are explored. Our capacity to become more ourselves in Christ is continually increased. Instead of a type of growth that is imposed by others or expected by them, each of us is growing to become more of the person God created us to be.

Mutuality

The experience of unconditional acceptance is essential in the formation of who we are in Christ. However, one of the paradoxical dynamics of salugenic relationships is that acceptance does not continue long term to be unconditional. Each person must begin to contribute to the life of the group by giving as well as receiving.

We need look no further than Christ's ministry to see that He did not always accept people unconditionally. The Pharisees, for example, often felt insulted by His words to them (Luke 11:45). Even though Peter was one of the inner group of disciples, Jesus rebuked him publicly (Mark 8:33). It seems that although Christ offered unconditional acceptance at times, there were other times when He appeared quite intolerant of sin.

In our own congregation and ministry we have noticed a pattern. For an initial period of time the person would be accepted unconditionally. Any unhelpful behavior would be excused and absorbed as they were given the opportunity to discover what kind of a church it was and time to begin to build relationships. However, after somewhere between six and twelve months, depending on the individual, a different dynamic would begin. Acceptance would become increasingly conditional.

Conditional acceptance among a group of people who are in a salugenic relationship together relates to the willingness of each person to accept the other and to accept the priorities of the group. If, after a period of time, an individual persists in a selfish way of life that is perceived to harm other members of the group, they no longer continue to be accepted in an unconditional way. A most severe example of this principle in Scripture is that of Ananias and Sapphira (Acts 5).

In order for relationships to be salugenic, mutuality is essential. If any one member continues to want to remain solely in the role of recipient, the overall relationships of the group will become less and less salugenic. Of course, there are times when we all need support from someone more experienced, but we ourselves are also able to give support to someone less experienced than us. Likewise, if a member insists on reaching out to others without allowing others to reach out to them, the balance of mutuality will be lost.

The perichoretic dynamic of divine community is the epitome of mutuality. We are suggesting that in the body of Christ we all both give and receive. Every member must play their part, and when anyone does not, it is a drain on all the others and will change the efficacy of the group.

Implications for Relationships

Being accepted is a powerful experience. When we give ourselves permission to be accepted by others, it will connect with the very deepest yearning of our hearts. It is an experience every human being both desires and should have. Sadly, many have not known it. Some continue to seek it; others have resigned themselves to not knowing it.

Acceptance is something every salugenic community can practice. It is always a challenge, however, to keep the experience of acceptance mutual. Most of us are more accustomed to slip into the role of either giver or receiver than to allow ourselves to both give and receive in the same set of relationships. Salugenic relationship has to be learned over time. It comes naturally to very few of us. For many of us, the best we can manage is to be part of one group where we offer acceptance to others and perhaps another where we allow ourselves to receive acceptance. The exertion of living both dynamics creates a range of very complex demands on all members. We have to gently challenge one another to move away from the roles we are most comfortable with.

Discovering an acceptance that does not condone sin is also a challenge. When we first come to Christ, none of us has the capacity to leave behind all our damage in a moment. Communities would be empty if we all had to be perfect. So salugenic communities include the damage that we bring. Yet even while we are becoming aware of the sin that we need to confess and give to Christ, we still require the ongoing acceptance from others that supports us in knowing that it is worth continuing.

The dynamic that makes this culture or environment possible is the ongoing evidence that each person is committed to this journey of transformative change. If you see someone beginning to change, you know that it is only a matter of time before the areas of damage that are the most difficult for you will also begin to shift in their life. This often requires some change from each of us as we love the other while their sin still impacts our own unresolved hurts.

It is also almost impossible to offer what we haven't ourselves known to those we don't yet trust or like. Prior to experiencing life-changing acceptance, we cannot offer it. Our capacity to offer acceptance lags behind our experience of it. So there is a sense in which acceptance is never wholly mutual. Newer members of the community will have less ability to offer acceptance. But if the expectation of mutual acceptance is clearly stated, the desire to grow the ability to offer acceptance can then be encouraged.

In the absence of mutual acceptance, journeys of ongoing change are much harder to undertake. Which of us wants to take a personal risk, to move into uncharted territory, among those who we know already have reservations about who we are? Likewise, it is impossible to have an experience of being one with others who have not accepted us. Oneness requires acceptance, recognition, and experience of mutual worth and value. Our suggestion, therefore, is that discovering how to live in mutual acceptance is a precursor to a consistent experience of journeying together into greater wholeness and Christlikeness.

Such a journey needs to be an intentional exploration of supernaturally given love among a group of people who each commit to living it with one another. It will inevitably expose both to ourselves and to others those parts of us that we find hardest to accept about ourselves since these are the areas that we react to most strongly in others. Simply by seeking to live together in a giving and receiving of acceptance, our own personal journey of growth will be encouraged, supported, and more focused.

To Consider

For you:
- What has been your most significant experience of unconditional acceptance?
- Which aspect of your own uniqueness do you want to explore further?
- What are the most helpful ways of communicating to someone else that you require a growing mutuality from them?
- Who do you find most difficult to accept? What can you do to ensure that you can feel and communicate God's love for them while remaining graciously intolerant of any damage they may be doing to you or others?

For your group:
- Who is the most difficult kind of visitor for your community to offer acceptance to? Why is this? What are you going to do about it?
- Which member of your group is likely to feel most insignificant? What can you do about this?
- How does your group want to respond when someone wishes to receive acceptance but doesn't want to adapt their behavior to the needs of the group?

CHAPTER 12

Choice

We can now move on to another facet of salugenic relationship. It is encapsulated in that simple word "choice." This is the self-selected element in transformative change.

From a biblical perspective choice is part of the very foundation of God's relationship with us as human beings. He gave us free will. When God said to Adam that he was not to eat from the tree of the knowledge of good and evil (Genesis 2:17), He still gave Adam the choice. Adam could obey God's instruction or disobey it and suffer the consequences. Adam and Eve decided to exercise their free will and chose to disobey God. Likewise, we, too, have the choice. We can choose who we will become, whether we will obey God and receive blessing or follow our own way and bring damage into our lives and into the lives of others (Exodus 20:5; Deuteronomy 28:32).

It would have been much easier for God if He had removed from Adam and Eve the power of choice, but He chose not to. Likewise, it is much easier for us to reduce the opportunities for choice open to those around us. Our societies are increasingly moving toward a policy of imposing healthy lifestyles (for example, bans on smoking in certain places). Our schools, likewise, are minimizing the power to choose how to express religion (banning head-scarves, for instance, or certain types of assemblies). In our churches we have expectations of what the Christian life should look like. When some choose to deviate from our norms, our comfort zones are challenged.

If we are to encourage transformative change in our congregations and small groups, that change is not one that can be imposed. Individuals must be given the power to choose. This is more radical than it sounds, so let us look at four aspects of choice in a salugenic community where choice has become a reality.

Being Allowed to Choose

When people came to the Son of God, it is quite remarkable that He allowed them to choose how to respond to Him. He could have underscored His comments with innuendo and added a bit of manipulation so that people felt little freedom to walk away. He could have called on all the powers of heaven to force people to accept His authority. Instead, it seems He went to great lengths to give them the power to choose for themselves how they wanted to respond to Him.

Think of the parables. Jesus used a narrative style that would have been quite familiar to the people of His day. They weren't used to an intellectual presentation of an argument. They learned from stories handed down through many generations (Deuteronomy 4:9; Psalm 44:1). However, many of the stories Jesus told were somewhat ambiguous. Jesus, it seems, taught certain truths in a deliberately vague and unclear fashion (ideas, Matthew 5.1ff.; parables, Matthew 13:1–23, etc.).

We would like to suggest that one of the reasons why Jesus taught in this way was to safeguard people's power to choose. His manner and His teaching forced people to make their own choices. They could walk away, perhaps to come back later? Or they could commit themselves to following Him and acting in obedience to His suggestions. No doubt some hovered on the fringes of His circle of friends and followers, only choosing to be involved much later, with the growth of the early church. By their choice they would earn the right to understand the parables and teach what He taught.

In our churches it is often hard to protect people's personal power to choose. For instance, do they have the freedom to come one week and not the next? Or do you feel the need to tell them you missed them last week? Can they leave after being in leadership and then come back a year or two later and still be welcomed—without being judged? How are folk viewed if they choose to dress differently or they begin to exercise an area of gifting or ministry in the local community that is particularly unusual and perhaps apparently antisocial? What if they want to come to church but do not want to explore a personal faith—are they still welcome?

We each have the opportunity and the privilege of giving the power of choice to those around us. We can give them the freedom to make their own choices, even if they are choices we wouldn't make for ourselves or choices that we don't think are necessarily wise. What matters is not what we think, or even what we think God thinks, about those choices! What is important is that we respect the individual's God-given free will so that they are allowed to choose for themselves, in their time and in their way.

Carrying Personal Responsibility

One of the consequences of being given the power to choose is that then each of us really does carry personal responsibility for our own choices. Being given the choice makes it much harder to abdicate that responsibility. It is ours to carry.

Once again, in Christ's ministry we see clearly that He did not allow people to evade responsibility. As we have already noted, He made it plain that He expected people to ask (Matthew 8:2; Luke 8:41). Even if He could see they were in need, even if they knew He knew what the need was, He still required that they openly, publicly, declare their need (Luke 18:40). This was not because Christ didn't know what they wanted. It was because the act of asking was in itself a significant step in their journey of transformative change.

Adam and Eve were given numerous responsibilities. One of Adam's first duties was to name the animals. God brought them to him to "see what he would name them" (Genesis 2:15, 19). In our churches we have slipped into a mindset of asking God what He wants. We want to know what God's will is for everything, and in one sense this is absolutely right. But God did not tell Adam what names He thought were best for the animals. Adam had to take some responsibility for his own choice. So do we, even today!

Carrying responsibility for another person is a burden. It is one reason why the burnout rate in pastoral care is so high.[1] Even in day-to-day relationships in churches there are those who seem to expect others to be responsible for them. After all, aren't we paying them to look after us? In times of need all of us need others to step in and guide us and perhaps even carry us for a time, but this should always be temporary. We must each be willing to be responsible for ourselves and also have the freedom not to be responsible for others. One of the phrases often heard in our work is, "I will leave it with you," implying, of course, that you will not carry an ongoing responsibility for the other person.

Making Mistakes

One of the uncomfortable realities about giving people choices is that the choices they make will often be unwise. Whether in a deliberate act of defiance or simply out of inexperience or ignorance, we all make mistakes. Think about the number of mistakes that surrounded Christ's ministry. Peter began to sink instead of successfully walking on water (Matthew 14:29–30) and had that embarrassing moment when Jesus rebuked him by saying, "Get behind me, Satan!" (Mark 8:33). The disciples squabbled about who was the greatest (Mark 9:33–34), and James and John wanted pride of place in the kingdom (Mark 10:35–37). How often did the disciples try to turn away those who Christ was about to minister to? How often did they demonstrate their inexperience by being unable to heal those who came to them?

Christ could have adopted a completely different strategy. It might be argued that in some ways it would have been more responsible to have made their learning and growing a far simpler and slower exercise. Sending them out two by two when they had been with Him for only a year or so (Mark 6:7) was a risky, almost irresponsible thing to do. To have schooled them and tested them, waiting until their competence was beyond doubt, and then sent them out would surely have guaranteed a higher success rate—or would it?

The truth is that any successful journey of change is full of mistakes. By God's grace they will all only be small ones and easily corrected, but they are mistakes, nonetheless. Which of us learned to walk without falling over a few times? Yet today we struggle to give people in our congregations the choice to make mistakes. Our journey of transformative change requires an environment where it is safe to make mistakes, to learn from them, and then not to repeat them (too often!).

Participation

This aspect of choice relates not to the person's own journey of transformative change, but instead to the way that the group or local church operates. We will see later that all the characteristics we are describing have to be embodied at each level of congregational life. This is especially true of choice.

In an environment that enables transformative change, the exercise of choice by each participant is both personal and relational within the context of the group. Members are together actively involved in making decisions, influencing direction, etc. Instead of the organization being formed around the wishes of a few key leaders, everyone has the opportunity to guide it. Of course, not all participate and contribute in the same way. Uniqueness means that some will want to be very involved in decision making, while others will find that it is the day-to-day activities of the group that are the focus of their participation. But any can choose to develop their participation in any direction, if they so wish. In the context of an organization, choice means that the responsibility for the organization is shared widely among its members, in a democratic way. Each person will know that their choice about how the organization should run will be respected and remain influential.

If some view themselves as less significant than others in the organization, their willingness to exercise choice is dampened. The environment may continue for a while to be one that changes them, but for them it is becoming more one way. The environment is no longer being changed by their involvement and presence within it. Over the course of time this can have an adverse impact on their own journey of transformative change.

This perspective on mutual participation also has implications for leadership structures and the distribution of power in an organization. It means that the organizational hierarchy is likely to be flatter, as there is no room for autocrats. Those with leadership responsibility will seek out the opinions of others and delegate and train others as much as possible. The goal will be an empowering of others' choices.

Implications for Relationships

Being part of a group where choice is a core value is risky, especially if we also expect others in the group to grow and change. What if the choices that are important to me are the ones that others change? Group life is much more straightforward if the number of choices available to members is limited.

At the heart of the question of choice is the fundamental belief that it is helpful, perhaps even essential, for each person to make their own choices about as many things as possible, rather than to be dictated to by others. This suggests a measure of trust in each person's capacity to choose or to recognize when they need advice and support in making a choice. The ability to make these choices is part of wholeness, part of the growing image of God in us.

The dynamics of relationships are changed when choice is so fundamental that we prioritize it even if this means that decisions are made in an apparently less-than-efficient way. If you are the most experienced member of a group, you may know the most helpful way for the group to deal with a particular trauma or challenge. But is it more important to tell them, so that the process can be trouble free, or to give group members a series of choices and let them work their way through their own clumsy learning journey?

When we feel we have the mind of God on a matter, giving other people choices becomes even more difficult. Scripture may be so abundantly clear, or we may have heard God's voice so irrefutably, that we know we can confidently give the person or the group clear direction. In salugenic relationships, however, where we are prioritizing the growth of the other people, supporting them as they exercise their own choice will in most cases lead to greater long-term fruit than an imposed wisdom. Christ rarely chose the simple option for the disciples.

Allowing mistakes creates the same kind of challenge. Which is of more value—to prevent mistakes altogether or to be forgiving and supportive when mistakes occur? Of course, much depends on the nature of the mistake, its consequences, and who will be affected. So there can be no strict rule. But as a general principle, Christ seems to have created situations where the disciples made their mistakes in front of one another. He then used each mistake as a learning curve, when more damage was exposed and more growth stimulated. This approach is counterintuitive and feels less safe yet seems to be the way God often works.

To Consider

For you:

* What is the area of choice in which you feel most restricted at the

moment? What would be the most helpful way of handling this?

- Think of a mistake someone has made recently. How can you communicate acceptance despite that mistake?
- What area of your life do you find it hardest to take responsibility for? What can you do to grow in that area?

For your group:

- What can you do to make it easier for mistakes to be talked about in constructive ways?
- Who are the most influential people in your group? Who are the least influential? What can you do about this?

CHAPTER 13

Openness

Openness is the third of our characteristics that help precipitate transformative change. Openness is about the willingness to be seen as we really are, without hiding away the parts of ourselves that we fear would be most unacceptable.

More than most this characteristic represents quite a challenge to the life of any group. It is part of our human nature to be selective about what we say and to whom we say it. For instance, if we are with a group of musicians, we are more likely to talk about aspects of our lives that relate to music rather than to sports or technology. We all tend to focus on that which we have in common. This is a perfectly natural and healthy part of communication. Being totally open or transparent is not part of normal, everyday life in any relationship.

However, this tendency to share the most acceptable parts of us means that we inevitably tend to hide the parts that we believe to be least acceptable. Perhaps we are less than honest about our opinions, preferring to be seen having opinions that won't cause offense. Alternatively, we might have parts of our lives that we don't mention because of our shame at our mistakes.

In an environment that is going to encourage transformative change, participants choose to make a commitment to be open about who they are, warts and all! There is no hiding. In the midst of mutual acceptance, we speak and live more openly than we might otherwise be comfortable with. It is a choice, of course, though if too many people choose to stop being so open, then the dynamic of group life becomes less transformative.

Again, this characteristic is consistently found throughout Christ's ministry. His very presence seemed to provoke greater honesty in some, bringing to light what had been hidden. Think of the possessed man who challenged Christ in the synagogue at Capernaum and ended by being released and healed (Luke 4:31–37). Likewise, Christ drew from the woman at the well an increasing measure of truth about her relationships with men. It is as though He had around Him an anointed force field and anyone stepping up to it was challenged to be more honest and transparent.

We are not suggesting that this is some magical power. As we learn from Christ's ministry, it is part of the work of the Holy Spirit to bring truth to us (John 16:13). Traditionally, the assumption has been that this is truth about the world around us, relationships, the future, and God's perspective. But within a salugenic setting it is also the work of the Holy Spirit to bring us more truth about ourselves, from His perspective. Sometimes we need the help of the Holy Spirit to connect with levels of honesty that we would otherwise avoid, have little knowledge of, or be unwilling to share. Scripture is clear that this same dynamic should be at work in our relationships with one another. See 1 John 1, for example, where living in light with one another, as God is light, also means being willing to confess our sins to one another.

Let us suggest four aspects to openness in the context of congregational life.

Being Real

At the heart of the practice of being open is the willingness of participants in a group to "be real" with one another. There are different ways of describing this level of interaction. Some call it authenticity, others simply straight talking, taking off a mask, or being yourself. Many do actually find it a relief to be able to "let out" every part of who they are without feeling the need to conform. But getting to the place of being so open will be a battle for each and every one of us. It takes time to enter such a deep openness with others.

Being real also means that each participant is willing to adopt a level of honesty that might not be welcomed in other environments.

In particular, it means acknowledging to others our own weaknesses, sharing mistakes, and, as we noted above, confessing sin and baggage to one another. One of the outcomes is the creation of a level of mutual vulnerability. But even though each person may have the power to mock, undermine, or hurt another member of the group, each chooses not to.

In one of his better-known books, social psychologist Erving Goffman reports on a study of village life in a community on the Shetland Isles, north of Scotland. Commenting on his findings, he suggests that we each choose a "self" to present to one another on the basis of what we think is going to be most acceptable.[1] It is like being on a stage, he says, with others as an audience.

We are suggesting in this book that when we are in an environment that encourages us to "be real," we bring a far greater proportion of who we are to each encounter. Every part of who we are becomes acceptable. So we can present to others in our group even the parts that we might be ashamed of. Some we may be desperate to change; others we may not be ready to address. The group members together will be able to carry this for one another.

Jesus' view on such matters is most explicit in His dealings with the Pharisees. He was clear that He felt they placed an emphasis on outer behavior, on playing to their audience. Yet what God looks upon and values is the inner person, below the water line, that which is not normally seen. In an environment that encourages transformative change, the inner part of us, hidden from us and from others, is brought out into the open by the requirement that we "be real." If we then do not like what we see about ourselves, it gives us a greater capacity to change.

Being real in a congregational setting has particular challenges for the expression of faith. The implication is that if you are having a difficult time in your relationship with God, you would be able to speak about this freely. If someone discovers they are angry at God, there would be an appropriate opportunity to admit this and talk about it without condemnation. Likewise, for those who haven't yet made a decision about their faith, or who are experiencing a time of doubt, openness means this can be freely talked about, rather than making a pastoral appointment and discussing it behind closed doors.

The Idea of Holistic Personhood

One of the consequences of openness and its transparency is that every part of our personhood and every area of our lives are, of necessity, involved. There is no taboo, no area outside this transparency. Openness is holistic; like transformative change, it engages every aspect of our personhood.

One of the most challenging areas to include in congregational life is our emotion. Openness requires that we should be honest emotionally, with ourselves and with others, whereas many of us are more comfortable keeping our feelings private. In a salugenic community, if we want to weep, we can. If we want to dance or kneel in worship in response to what we are feeling, then we can. Likewise, if we have few feelings at the time, or find ourselves unable to respond, we are also free not to express any emotion.

When we are living in an environment of openness with others we are forced to be open both to ourselves and to the group about what is really going on inside us. We are no longer able to compartmentalize our attitudes and behavior. The discipline of the group imposes a unity and a consistency both within each of us individually and in our relationships. This helps stimulate a more holistic approach toward transformative change.

We call one another to be fully present. We call out from one another all that is hidden. The Lord can see what stands in His path, what resists His deeper intimacy with us. The discipline of others standing with us and the ability of God to see everything and bring it, by the Holy Spirit, to our and to others' notice guarantee that we approach this whole journey in a holistic way.

Organizational Responsiveness

Openness is another characteristic that extends into the way a group is run, as well as into the nature of the relationships in it. Openness in an organization relates very directly to its leadership structure, to how the organization is run, and to how decisions are made. It is an area that is a challenge for many churches. Where does the power lie? Whose voice speaks loudest? Whose interests are most protected in the decision-making process? A group with openness as a core value will have the means to review these questions often and to respond more spontaneously to both the vulnerable and the unheard.

In addition to making an impact on the way power is distributed and implemented, openness also means that the organization itself is responsive to the change that is occurring within it. Imagine an environment in which transformative change among the members is a priority. Such change will mean that within, say, three months there will be significant new dimensions to relationships, and out of these relationships will come numerous new initiatives and ideas. Things are guaranteed to happen that will ensure that a number of people within the organization will be different in some way from who they were before. How should the organization respond?

Jesus suggests a way forward by making a comparison between the use of old and new wineskins for new wine (Mark 2:22). Old wineskins have no capacity to respond flexibly. The skin is not supple, so therefore cannot expand during the fermenting process. Instead, the skin will split, with the result that the wine will be lost. New wineskins, by contrast, are able to be far more responsive to the maturing process of the wine. The expanding of the wineskin is a response to the ongoing and changing needs of the wine.

Similarly, even though the structures and traditions of an "old wineskin" organization may be deeply valued and have been very effective in the past, this may not continue to be the case. If old structures cannot respond with honor and flexibility to the emergence of new ideas and initiatives, then they will quickly become resistant to the transformative change going on within them. If an organization wants to enable the processes of transformative change, it must expect to be changed by the dynamic within it.

Protecting Confidentiality?

One of the challenges that any group has to address if it is to live with openness is the challenge of protecting confidentiality while encouraging people to be open. It is important that people should always feel that they have some control over the boundaries of their own lives. Confidentiality and respect for individual privacy can contribute to that in a helpful and positive way.

However, confidentiality can also be quite threatening and become obstructive to transformative change. Have you ever been in a situation where someone says to you, "I need to tell you something, but you need to promise not to tell anyone else"? The sentiment expressed is the antithesis of openness. It can create both a barrier to deeper relationships and an opportunity for subversive pockets of seemingly justifiable concealment.

The other difficulty is that many are today claiming absolute secrecy. This is especially true in the United States. In salugenic relationships people have to learn that speaking more openly about a matter is essential to breaking its power over their lives. For none of us can celebrate breakthrough or greater wholeness if we are not prepared to talk openly about the damage in our lives.

A further dimension is the fact that the power of the Enemy is very much reinforced when matters are allowed to remain secret. What is hidden cannot be cleansed. Therefore, following Christ's practice of bringing into the public arena what had been hidden (in His conversation with the woman at the well, for example, and the healing of the woman suffering from bleeding, Luke 8:42–48), in our salugenic communities, we, too, must begin to practice "confession."

In salugenic relationships there is mutual confidentiality within a group, and group members will not betray a confidence by talking to people outside the group, but no one person can require confidentiality of another to the exclusion of the group. In speaking openly there should be nothing to fear, for the group is learning to forgive one another's mistakes, to value uniqueness, and to support one another as they speak openly about what was formerly hidden. In that sense, all of us have secrets that we need to speak openly about.

These questions become a little clearer when other characteristics are also applied. Both parties in the interaction need to be given choice, in order to protect the openness. The person who has something to share must be given the option not to share it. But, likewise, the person who is about to be told the secret must have permission to then tell an appropriate other person if they feel that is necessary. For instance, if a person confesses to being sexually abused, and it is possible the abuser could still be abusing others, then the matter must be taken further. Absolute confidentiality is rarely mutually beneficial in lay relationships.

Implications for Relationships

The decision to practice openness with others requires courage. However, the vulnerability of openness is less risky because of the mutuality of the relationships. Each member has an equal measure of power over the other. Yet it still feels like walking down Main Street or through a shopping mall with no clothes on. Adam and Eve were comfortable naked before the fall, but they felt driven to cover their nakedness once they were divided from God and from each other. Like them, we all instinctively want to avoid such transparency.

Inner change requires an uncomfortable measure of openness. All the hidden parts of us need to be brought into the light so they can be seen and dealt with. If they are good, they need not be hidden but can be celebrated. If they are rooted in damage, they need God's attention as part of our journey of growth. It is often the role of others to precipitate that growth by helping us face those inner parts of ourselves that we have lost contact with. For most of those who have entered such a group, things will seem worse before they get better. But better is guaranteed.

To Consider

For you:
- What parts of who you are do you keep most hidden?
- What would happen if you began to be more open about these parts of your life?
- What can you do to help others around you feel more able to be real when they are with you?

For your group:
- Which do you place least emphasis on: the cognitive, the emotional, the spiritual, or the social? What would happen if you began to develop the areas you emphasize least?
- Which area of your group life is most in need of change? How are you going to start?
- How effective is your balance between openness and confidentiality?
- Who might be disadvantaged by your changing this balance, and what can you do about this?

CHAPTER 14

In Summary

Creating an environment that consistently creates opportunities to meet Jesus together is not easy. We have explored three qualities—acceptance, openness, and choice—that help enable transformative change to happen in a local congregation or small group. These are relational qualities that create room for change to occur. They change the flavor of relationships. What had been threatening and full of imposed expectations is a space in which love and growth can flourish.

Christ's relationships were full of these qualities. How others responded to them determined the direction of the relationship, but His offer of salugenic relationship was always consistent. It would be nice to say that as we grow in our wholeness, we will have greater capacity to offer these relationships to others. Though this is indeed true, it is also true that rather than waiting, we have first to build these relationships, and benefit from them mutually, in order to discover more of the very wholeness we need to live them!

Part 5
RELATIONSHIPS ON THE MOVE

We have considered the core qualities of relationships that enable salugenic community. But focusing on those qualities themselves is rarely effective. While making room for acceptance, choice, and openness, our focus must remain on the journey toward Christlikeness.

RELATIONSHIPS THAT EMBODY ACCEPTANCE, CHOICE, AND OPENNESS are, for most of us, hard to find. They are experiences fundamental to the very expression of our God-given humanity, yet they are almost impossible to achieve with any degree of consistency. They are, however, the type of foundation that most people need in order to risk significant personal change. Few of us have ever known them.

Part of the reason why these values are so problematic is that there are times when they conflict with one another. Imagine a group where one person has an asthmatic condition and another person is a smoker. In the exercising of choice, one will want to smoke, and the other will want a smoke-free atmosphere. They cannot both exercise choice freely in such a situation. Again, think of a group where one person is very angry with men, perhaps for good reason. That person wants to be "real" about that anger in a very forthright manner but, in doing so, might express their anger in a way that undermines the personal worth of the men in the group. Openness and acceptance conflict with each other.

These three values of acceptance, choice, and openness, with all that they encompass, can be in competition. Group life is therefore not as simple as devising a set of guidelines, or adopting several values, that can then be the foundation of relationships. Somehow these values have to be prioritized.

In choosing how the competing priorities of group life can operate, we must remind ourselves of the purpose of our relationships. This will help guide how we deal with the inevitable tensions and conflicts as each of us continues our journey of change. Whose choice is more important, the smoker or the asthmatic, the person feeling deeply angry or the person potentially hurt by the expression of the anger? These are very real questions and have to be considered in openness. When there is a clear and shared purpose, they can be successfully resolved.

In this chapter we will focus on the purpose of our relationships together and on the resources needed for that purpose to be successfully achieved.

CHAPTER 15

Journeying Together

J ourneying together is the fourth characteristic of congregational life that we will explore together. We would like to suggest that when Christ is in our midst, it is "journeying together" that expresses more clearly than any other characteristic the purpose of our relationships.

It is often too easy to be too specific. Let us explain. Some groups and congregations may say that the purpose of being together is specifically for each to become more like Christ. Others might be meeting to focus on a specific mission or need. They would still want to meet Jesus together, even if that is not their primary purpose. The difficulty is that the more specific you are about the journey you are focusing on, the more likely you are to exclude those who would express their journey in a different way.

In this book, therefore, we are simply describing the journey as a journey into wholeness. This will require a journey that encompasses personal growth for all who participate. Its destination is greater Christlikeness, and every step moves us closer to this. But it might be helpful in the short term to adopt language that we or others are more comfortable with. This is an important part of recognizing individual choice and in the long term need not dilute the process of journeying together.

A Common Goal—Transformative Change

For relationships to be effectively salugenic, a goal is needed, that is, a purpose. They must have a direction. As we have seen, this focus then becomes the means whereby decisions can be made about priorities in relationships. For those around Christ during His three-year ministry, the goal was consistently clear. He was teaching them God's perspective and showing them how to live their daily lives in ways that were more appropriate for followers of God. He expected that they were changed by His presence.

All of Christ's life was given over to this purpose—to His communicating the Father's perspective on His followers and on how they lived their lives. It culminated in His obedience at the cross. During His ministry He gathered those around Him who increasingly began to adopt this goal of living their lives as followers of God. His choices and decisions about what to teach, how to respond to questions, and who to spend time with were all guided by this goal. So, for instance, He never wasted time on peripheral issues or relationships that did not contribute to His own clear goal. Everything was governed by this priority in His life and ministry.

It is evident from Scripture that Christ was quite ruthless about this goal. Those for whom other aspects of daily life were more important went away disappointed after an encounter with Him. In His presence their conflicting loyalties were exposed, and until they had changed to accommodate His goals and priorities, they would not find their place among the group of those who were close to Him. His goal of making His Father known was so focused that anything else was dismissed.

Being with Jesus was being with God. Things got done; things changed; things were exciting. In a sense, this perspective and the way He lived it were exactly what the people around Him had all been waiting and looking for. Yes, they had found what they had been looking for. Being close to God by being around His Son was the part that had been missing from their lives.

Those who were around Jesus shared His purpose. To begin with, none of them fully realized what it was about Him that they found so irresistible. Only over time did they come to realize that they were giving up something in order to have something more valuable. In His presence His was the purpose that prevailed. Those who stayed with Him could assume that this was the underlying motivation for their being together, even though a number of them lost touch with that purpose at various times during His ministry (see, for example, John 6:59–71).

Christ seems to have consistently exposed those parts of each person's life that were not in accordance with His goal. He brought into the open that which hindered their greater intimacy with Him. Christ needed to clear the path of all baggage and debris. He being a bit like a bloodhound, the scent of it was clear to Him, and He pursued it. Being with Him meant giving Him permission to draw attention to such damage, while also welcoming His intervention so that the damage could be undone, thereby enabling greater maturity and growth.

Should we expect anything less today when Christ is present among us as we are gathered in twos and threes? Christ's priorities are unchanged. He calls us to grow in Him and to make Him known, to be disciples and make disciples. When we become aware of His presence together, we inevitably become aware of this priority, too. Likewise, when we also make this our priority, bringing God's perspective to one another in salugenic relationships, we inevitably welcome more of His presence. For this is the work of the Holy Spirit—to bring truth to us all.

But we must be careful. Some of those who met Christ were not specifically in search of a relationship with God or of God's perspective. This was not the journey they thought they were on. Some wanted healing, some needed forgiveness, and some didn't realize who they were about to meet. It was a goal they grew into. So it is today. What matters is that the relationships should have a common goal, a shared purpose and intent. For some salugenic relationships, it will be enough to want to grow and change and to have this as a common goal for the group, even if the nature of the change is quite distinct for each member. Christ has shown that He will meet each of us where we are and move us all to the place where He wishes us to be and become. Likewise, we, too, can do the same for one another.

When transformative change is part of the common goal, inclusion is maximized. This is the kind of goal that anyone who wants to grow can identify with. The only people it excludes are those who don't yet recognize that they need to change and those unwilling to do so. Everyone else, whatever journey of personal growth they may be on, can be included if they so wish. For being around others who are wanting to change will change us, to be more like Him. This is why Christ told us to go to the sick and the poor, for He knew they were the ones who were most likely to be willing to change in this way.

Sharing the Journey

There is another feature of the journey that is integral to the purpose of salugenic relationships. Yes, each of us is acknowledging our own desire to continue our journey of growing, changing, and becoming more Christlike. We have this desire in common. But we are also willing to share one another's journeys.

In our Western society, church has become quite individualistic, private, and even secret. Knowing God is a private, personal affair, pursued in relative isolation. We may know that a hundred or more others in our congregation are also pursuing a similar journey. We may even meet a small number of them from time to time to discuss a topic of interest or concern. But most of the time church life consists of, say, a hundred people each separately walking a (perhaps) similar journey in a relationship with God, but talking little about it to others and sometimes even less to those close to them.

Christ's principle of "where two or three are gathered" seems to run counter to this all too familiar experience of individual, private journeying. When He was among His disciples, there were countless times when He made one person's experience an experience that was shared with others. With Christ other people were present in even the most intimate of personal encounters.

How many of such shared-journey relationships do we really have? Or perhaps more pertinently, how many do we really want? As we have seen, it is a very vulnerable thing we do to ourselves when we invite someone to share intimately in our journey of growing and positively changing. For such change to take place, there must always be an element of loss of control, together with a depth of trust that leaves us exposed to being hurt. Many of us will have experienced betrayal in similar relationships in our past—so our immediate question will be: What guarantee do we have that it will not happen again?

Here we return to the three characteristics we identified earlier: acceptance, choice, and openness. The mutuality that they carry makes a shared journey possible. When we can experience being accepted and being treated by others as someone of worth, it becomes easier to trust their contribution to our ongoing transformative change. When we know that openness means we are allowed to choose, we can be more real, and when we know that we can make mistakes yet still be accepted, vulnerability does not feel such a fear-full thing. When we also know that the journey is mutual, and we are invited to support the other in the way they are supporting us, we can be more comfortable. Power and responsibility shared mutually are empowering, whereas power in the hands of an "other" creates the possibility of victims.

It is willingness to share the journey together that creates a common goal and makes meeting Jesus together more likely. The commonality of our shared attitude and commitment is experienced together as an intimate reality, instead of our merely paying lip service to a mission statement or a pious thought from a sermon. What we learn together on this journey is that Christ will take us as deep as we dare go, and journeying in this way we discover that this is what it is all about, that this is what we are created for—intimacy with divinity shared with others in humanity. We would like to suggest that this is part of what God intends in His emphasis on body life, the reality that Christ is present when two or three of us are together. Scripture suggests that we each need the other and that we meet this need by being together. For when we are together, we are better able to reflect God's image as divine community.

Rather than our individualistic private understanding of maturity, often including a significant element of independence, God's perspective seems different. Wholeness means the perichoresis of interdependence, me needing you and you needing me, each contributing to the life of the other. If I do not have you, I cannot fulfill my own mandate from God to be more like Him as divine community. So the more I do community together successfully, the more I reflect in myself the dynamic of social relational Trinity. We are in His image, but we all still have to grow into His likeness, to become more, by His grace and help, as He already is in His nature (1 John 3:3).

A Changing Community

There is also another aspect of our journeying together that has quite profound implications. Imagine that each person in your group is on a journey. You all have the same goal, although each of you expresses it in a slightly different way. Likewise, you all perceive yourselves to be in different places on that journey. The life of your group together is found in the mutual support you give one another on the next step. Imagine your group in a year's time. Each member has moved on, some radically, some gently, but all are now in a different place. What will have happened to the group?

If the group is to continue to prioritize supporting each of you on your respective journeys, it is inevitable that the group must itself continue to change. Perhaps one of those who was more experienced is now going through a difficult time. As they struggle to change themselves, for a while they have less to give. Perhaps half the members are being challenged by God to address family matters, whereas previously there was more focus on growing greater intimacy with Christ. Thus you find that the dynamic, direction, and even short-term priority of the group are different at different times on your journey together.

Many people yearn for this sense of a group that is on the move in itself. Goals are being achieved, prayers are being answered, and change is visibly successful. Yet such changes can also make us feel quite insecure. We are often more comfortable with static hierarchies, whether visible or invisible, than with a fluctuating network of relationships where contributions and commitments vary. We prefer stability, even stagnation, to change that is not under our control.

The Gospels give us the impression that there was an underlying, consistent unpredictability about Christ. His approach to each situation, each person, was new, even novel or eccentric. His answers, His requirements, and His expectations were often opposite to custom, or the norms of the day, and He was never afraid to say so. Consequently, at times He even came across as offensive. Christ brought a sense of originality, expectation, and even novelty to each encounter. The disciples never quite knew what was going to happen next. Although they could have confidence in His consistency, grace, and approachability, they were never sure what the outcome might be. Being around a person like that can always be a bit risky! But the disciples did not mind because they trusted Him. So it is with support groups that have Christ among them.

Unless you have been part of a salugenic group, where change is the norm, not just the exception, it is hard to imagine that it is one of the safest places on earth. Yes, being in a group where there is ongoing positive change is what life in Christ is all about. This is a place where the scenery is always changing, where the relationships remain exciting, and where one moment is followed by another that is even more different. It is safe when people are safe and changing. When things are static, any change is a threat, but where all is changing all the time you can relax in the moment since you are confident that it will soon change!

It is the greatest sadness to us that in much local church life people continue to fight to keep things the same, while the Lord will often be seeking to stir things up, one way or the other. Christ never attacked tradition, except where it was deceitful or undermining of God's values, but change was always at the heart of all that He did and taught. After Christ had spoken, things were never the same. Should we expect anything less in our journeying with one another in His presence? A fundamentally different dynamic in our time together will be created when we allow Him to move this way through us in one another.

Implications for Relationships

Let's be honest; we all like things that are important to us to stay consistent, to remain the same. There is something a little exposing about knowing that something is going to change, especially when we are not sure what form that change will take. It is certain, however, that when journeying together is the common purpose of a group of people, transformative change is guaranteed.

What one quickly learns in such groups is that change is messy and always seems to leave us exposed. We may welcome the freedom to change ourselves, but the freedom for others to change is often less welcome. What if they leave us behind? What if they turn against us when they have changed? What will happen to the group that is now such an important part of me? Everyone will have these concerns. In a salugenic community it is essential to talk openly about them. It is part of being real and of ensuring that each person is confident that their choice and the other's choice will be mutually respected.

Whatever the difficulties, when we grow accustomed to change as the norm, we are dissatisfied with anything less than this new and exciting way to live.

To Consider

For you:
* What would you most fear changing if you were part of a salugenic group?

- How would you need to change in order to welcome such change?
- Can you imagine ever feeling that ongoing positive change could be a good thing in your life?

For your group:

- How can you most inclusively express your common goal?
- What ground rules, if any, would you all agree regarding confidentiality and change?
- What are the fears you each carry, and how can you respond to them?

CHAPTER 16

Resources That Enable Change

In our exploration of the characteristics that create relationships where meeting Jesus together is more likely, we come now to a final and distinct area—the resources that make change possible.

As with so many of these characteristics, the next point seems obvious once it is made. Jesus' presence in our midst produces an opportunity and desire for change, so the group needs to provide the resources to make the change effective. But the obvious is so often not obvious until it is stated. Despite the apparent simplicity of this statement, it is striking how few churches actually prioritize providing resources to help people pursue a journey of discipleship change.

Many faith communities will focus heavily on activities and programs that involve a wide number of people and are devoted to biblical teaching, prayer, and service of others, but none of these necessarily helps achieve the type of change we are considering. In fact, in many situations these very activities, intended to promote Christian faith, can accidentally inhibit transformative change.

Suppose that salugenic change is one of the overt goals of your group. Perhaps, like us, you believe that when Christ's presence is acknowledged, the result will always be some kind of change. In order to make it easier for your group to welcome Him, you will therefore also have to make it easier for transformative change to occur. What are the resources that will help that to happen? How can you facilitate such a thing?

Know-how

Jesus spent much of His three-year ministry teaching. This was clearly a priority for Him. He did so formally, teaching the crowds. He did so more informally, in His day-to-day relationships with the disciples and His circle of friends, especially the women. He also taught them by sending them out on teaching and healing missions where they could gain experience (Luke 9:1–6, 10; 10:1–11, 17) and by having them around Him as He healed and ministered. The know-how He focused on was very practical and frequently a response to the day-to-day situations and questions He encountered. It was the kind of learning that, when it was grasped, led to change in people's lives.

None of this change was change for change's sake. All the change that took place in the lives of the disciples helped prepare them to represent Him once He had gone. They were apprentices who were learning how Christ did things. They learned by doing. Teaching was not the goal. It was the first step in the disciples' journey of learning to change to be like Him. All that Christ did with His disciples was geared toward this practical outcome.

In our churches we should be continuing this tradition. We should expect people to change, so we must teach them just as Jesus did. We must provide a multitude of different opportunities for people to learn how to live as Christ's representatives, to change to become more like Him. Some of our learning and understanding comes through listening to concepts and ideas. But some also comes through example and narrative, that is, through our willingness to listen to others' experiences and learn from them. Their mistakes can help prevent us from making our own! But much of the acquisition of know-how is only embedded in our lives as we have the chance to experience it, to live it relationally, either by being a part of the change in another person's life, or by experiencing it for ourselves.

Teaching people how to change is a challenge if you have not experienced that change yourself, or if it has happened, but you do not understand quite how. We need those in our local churches who specialize in teaching us how to change, explaining what to do when the change feels obstructed, and encouraging us to persevere when the change feels too challenging.

"Just tell me what to do" is a frequent cry. We meet so many who have been seeking change for years. But the change they are so hungry for eludes them. They do not have the know-how. If churches are to become places of transformative change, we must acquire this knowledge and learn how to disseminate it effectively. The expertise must be distributed throughout the group and learned by everyone together.

In our Western society the usual assumption is that know-how resides with those who have been appropriately trained. We feel secure among people whose expertise has been verified by those who are themselves experts in the field. In a church context, this creates a reliance on the pastor and the leader. It absolves many of us from the responsibility of taking up an expertise of our own. Christ, however, renounced the idea of hierarchies of power. It seems that He expected everyone not only to change but also to learn the basics in order to be equipped to share their experience with others.

We see Christ quite deliberately inviting people who had a lack of know-how, investing in them considerable training and experience, and then sending them out to share that experience with others. Their know-how was not academic, nor was it acquired through study. It was firmly rooted in what had happened to them, what they had seen, and what they had begun to practice. Christ sidestepped the people who believed that they themselves represented God's viewpoint, and went straight to those who were hungry for food, healing, or change—in essence, for relationship with Him.

This approach to disseminating know-how puts power in the hands of the people. Paul went further, mandating each of us to take responsibility for our own gifting, practicing it as we learn to take our place in the body of Christ. God, it seems, invests know-how in each one of us and expects us to build our own expertise and make it available to one another—a mutual giving and receiving in the spirit of the perichoretic harmony of the social Trinity.

This means, to put it bluntly, that we are each a resource in one another's journeys of change. It also means that when we withhold that resource, we are in danger of obstructing such change. But if we all row the boat in the same direction, each of us making our own contribution to the goal, change is more possible. The result is a Christ-centered oneness.

We have, of course, to make allowances for our different gifting and different ways of learning. They are just as unique as any other part of us.

In particular, there are often gender differences. Although there are plenty of exceptions, women generally tend to be more people oriented, focusing on relationships, and men more goal oriented, focusing on things and projects. This fundamentally affects how we learn. It is perhaps also true to say that some men believe that they know everything already, whereas many women acknowledge that they know nothing, so need to learn everything. These differences affect the kinds of resources we will need and how we respond to them. We will explain in more detail later why in small groups of salugenic relationships we have found it helpful to start with gender-distinct groups.

Evidence of Success

In addition to the shared know-how that propels our journeys of change, there is a further wonderfully easy resource that we see Christ using very frequently—visible success! Success is contagious.

Creating a culture that celebrates success is not difficult once transformative change is under way. Every local church or group can give time, on a regular basis, to offering people the opportunity to share the positive change they have recently experienced. Participants can also be encouraged to "gossip" the success in conversation with one another during the week, thereby raising the profile of the amazing things that will begin to happen. One person's success acts as a resource to encourage the next.

We see this pattern also in Jesus' ministry. When He healed, the crowds knew and understood the power of the change. No doubt that is one reason why so many more had the courage to seek healing. People talked about what they had seen at work in the lives of others. This same dynamic can begin to work very powerfully in our own groups.

The public celebration of success can be a problem for those who are struggling. It can cause division or feelings of marginalization and failure. One remedy to this problem is to celebrate a wide diversity of types of success. The success of someone taking the first step, perhaps a conversion experience, is often shared in a service or meeting, followed by someone with their story of a more remarkable step, for example, a physical healing. But what of an experience of suddenly being able to forgive where in the past this wasn't possible or finding that the emotional pain of bullying or rejection has gone? If emphasis is placed on these apparently smaller steps of change, the consequences will be less divisive.

We should note, however, that speaking of successful change is something very different from those statements of "faith" that we make from time to time where the change has not yet happened. In our ministry we meet many whose declarations of success come close to denials of the reality, which is that the real situations are clearly fundamentally unchanged. Sharing success must be accompanied by "being real." If the problem hasn't gone yet, then it simply hasn't gone, and no one should feel they need to say otherwise. It is a sad fact that people can feel under pressure to say things that are not entirely true. Beware.

Sharing success should be an effective resource in several different ways. For the person who is making the declaration, it can act as a turning point. They are publicly acknowledging the change that has happened, leaving behind all of its history, and stepping into their future. But more significantly, sharing success can increase the possibility that others will also be stirred up to pursue the same kind of change. Expectations are heightened and sin is exposed when a testimony is authentic and resonates with others.

Of course, sharing success isn't done only with words. In our own groups, success is perhaps experienced as a resource most powerfully when lives are seen to be different—the person really is changing. For instance, you can see from a person's face that the anger has gone; or when someone starts a new training program, you know that the fear of failure that has dogged their steps for decades is at last undone. Again, as someone exercises their spiritual gifting for the first time, the growth in their relationship with God is plain for all to see. Such life change must be celebrated with the wider community, and when it is, the resource it offers for transformative change is significant.

Mutual Support

Our final type of enabling resource is the nature of the relationships among the group. There needs to be a tangible commitment that provides mutual support.

In our Western society the responsibility of providing support is given to specific groups of individuals: nurses, social workers, doctors, caregivers, to name but a few. These professions are essential, and we would not question their importance in society. But in our churches it is the responsibility of the pastoral team or the leadership to give such support. Or is it? In a salugenic community it is the responsibility of every member to be willing to provide support to others; it is not just the prerogative of the professional team or the trained man or woman of God. Mutual support is similar to the shared provision of know-how. It is a valuing of our own expertise. The difference is that although know-how does rely on expertise, whether gained by training or by experience, support is often simply the provision of love, care, and availability.

Have you noticed how many of the groups we are in have unofficial hierarchies, where each person knows their place? In these groups, those who are more experienced tend to provide more of the support. This can be good and right, as those with least experience are under no expectation to provide support to anyone else. But these hierarchies can also be roadblocks that prevent others from gaining experience. Once they are established, it is very difficult to challenge or change them. Those who have been in a group longer than you will always be in that group longer than you. There is no way you can overtake them. So the most experienced always remain the most experienced, and little effort is made to encourage the natural or intuitive gifting that may lie latent in the group.

The principle of mutual support runs counter to this hierarchical assumption. The starting point in a salugenic community is that each person commits to making a contribution to the support of others. In such a group no one has the luxury of simply receiving support without giving back, and no one has the luxury, as leader, of being the only one to give, rather than receive, support. Such identities are unhelpful and false in salugenic groups, and certainly do not reflect the reality of the journey to which all the group members are committed.

It is a challenge when you yourself are feeling vulnerable to pay attention to the vulnerability of another. Many times we would rather take the easier route and simply allow ourselves to remain on the receiving end. Similarly, if we know we are not ready to face an issue, it is easier to be the one who gives to others, rather than to be real enough to acknowledge that we are facing a logjam in our own journey. In a salugenic community where each person is committed to their own and others' journeys, there will be the opportunity gently to challenge these boundaries so that more growth can occur in all members of the group.

Implications for Relationships

Any kind of journey needs resources. That may be transport or food and drink. It may be a map or communication en route. Some journeys need extra preparation, and some may take surprising turns. The responses of your fellow travelers, and their actions, whatever they may be, also directly impact your experience of your own journey. Our journey together into wholeness is no exception. To be effective, it needs just as many resources. Many of us have tried to pursue such journeys with prayer, Bible study, and by listening to good preaching. These are important. But the resources that are needed for change to take place are often slightly different.

A salugenic community needs know-how, evidence of success, and mutual support. But without any leadership, where are these resources to come from? With Christ in our midst, they will come from Him and from each member as each contributes a little more than they feel able to. Each member must also be willing to receive from others a little more than they may be comfortable with. Expanding our boundaries is what salugenic community is all about.

To Consider

For you:
- Is giving or receiving more comfortable to you?
- What can you do to create opportunities to begin practicing and sharing resources, such as know-how, evidence of success, and mutual support?
- What would most need to change in you before you could comfortably stand up and talk about an area of success in your journey?

For your group:
- What would need to change in your community in order to make these resources more widely available?
- How would members react if they began to hear stories of change in people's lives?
- How would you know if someone was speaking the truth about the way they claimed to be changing?

CHAPTER 17

In Summary

The successful journeying of those who participate has to be at the core of relationships in a salugenic community. The responsibility for that success lies with every member. Christ will bless and supernaturally enhance it, but the initiative must be the combined effort of each person.

Real, tangible success is essential. For too long many of us have become accustomed to living more by faith than reality. We may try to declare boldly that we are changed, but the truth in our lives is often rather different. We may create the appearance of a journey of ongoing wholeness, but when we get close to others in an unfamiliar context, we feel uncomfortable. We are often afraid of people's reactions when we, or they, share.

Christ does not ask us to either fake or pretend on our journeying. Those who came to Him were not so ashamed of their need that they hid it under a guise of success. Likewise, as we learn the together part of this journey, our personal commitment to the goal of wholeness will become mingled with the commitment of others. Their change becomes our change, and together we become more Christlike.

Someone looking on from one week to the next will notice something unusual. It will not be that there is no leadership but rather that the leadership is shared among a significant number of the community. In a small community (for example, a small group) all members will participate in making a significant contribution. In a larger community (for example, a church) it may be that there are clearly identifiable leaders. But if that same someone were to look on a year later, they would observe that some of those leaders had become those who were receiving support and that a whole new generation of leaders had emerged.

Part 6
WHEN THE SALUGENIC IS CREATED

The qualities that we have described so far are wonderful. But they do not necessarily create a salugenic community. Though they may be present in individual relationships, something more has to happen for a group of people to be effectively salugenic. In this next section we will look at the transformative change that the group itself needs to go through in order to move from simply being a collection of individuals to becoming a salugenic community, consistently meeting Jesus together.

IMAGINE A CHURCH OR GROUP THAT HAS SALUGENIC characteristics as its core set of values. It is easy to see how it would be a popular place. You are spurred on in a journey that you have chosen, a journey that involves your own growth and development. You are surrounded by others who are pursuing their journeys, all in unique ways, yet with similar priorities to yourself. You know you are important to them, and you likewise value them for who they are.

It is a challenging environment. You are encouraged to be open about your fears and weaknesses, as others are also. It gets uncomfortable, perhaps, when your perspectives are exposed by the cut and thrust of interactions with others. But to your surprise you discover that you are not who you thought yourself to be and that you need to mature in your communication and other relationship skills. The practice of becoming more present when you are with others feels risky but is fulfilling when you achieve it.

At times, others ask you for support, and this can be annoying, but you know that you yourself benefited from something similar a week earlier and that the life of the group is made up of give as well as take. Whether you like it or not, you are beginning to be a giver as well as a taker. You can see others a little more experienced than you who seem to thrive on mutual giving and receiving as a way of life.

This community is also a place where nothing seems to stand still, and that is sometimes wearing. You meet a friend you haven't seen for a few weeks, and something feels different about them. You are not even sure you are comfortable with it, but they seem to be. They tell you they are working on an area of fundamental change in their life. You hesitate—this is not an area you have worked on yourself. How will the change in them affect the friendship you have? Only time will tell.

The disciples of Christ, and the early church, must have experienced very similar dynamics. There was incessant movement and change around Christ. Coming out of paganism or one of the cults would have demanded huge change. Christ was so full of surprises that His followers would barely have caught their breath before the next challenge was upon them. What would God do next? What would it mean for them?

The salugenic characteristics we explored in the previous two chapters are an important foundation upon which to create these kinds of dynamics in our relationships with one another. We think of them as the raw ingredients. But in order for a salugenic community to be created, something more needs to happen. It is not enough to have a mission statement that focuses on transformative change or to write acceptance, choice, and openness into the policies and preach these values on a Sunday. They have to be lived day to day.

We have all been in environments that pay lip service to these characteristics and perhaps even practice them on a piecemeal basis. Yet the presence of Christ is often not a reality in our midst in the way that we are describing here. Oneness may be a belief, but is not yet a genuine experience. Transformative change is something we might hear about from time to time, but it is not a common experience among everyone in the community.

So how do these ingredients turn into a cake? How do we move from practicing the characteristics in our relationships together to experiencing the oneness that unleashes the presence of Christ in the way that both Scripture and the salugenic community offer? We may create the opportunity for relationships to be salugenic. We may create space for transformative change to occur. But is that enough?

What we are suggesting in this book is that something more has to happen. It is something invisible, something slightly mystical. It is experienced, rather than being merely a decision. It is felt, rather than taught. It is real, rather than hoped for. It is obvious when you step into the room, rather than having to be announced in the notices or sermon. It is elusive, rather than tangible. It is the joint contribution of everyone, rather than being focused around a charismatic leader. One of the most intuitive ways of describing it is that it has a different "atmosphere."

CHAPTER 18

Creating an Atmosphere

Think of an environment where the participants consistently meet Jesus together. Suppose you were a visitor having your first contact with this group of people. You have stepped into one of their meetings. You find that it has a different atmosphere. Instead of simply being a collection of individual characteristics, there has been a blending of them all, a synergy has taken place, and something new has been created.

Atmosphere is a figurative term, of course. We are not referring to the combination of oxygen and carbon dioxide that contributes to our physical atmosphere. Nor are we referring to the addition of any particular perfume or scent, the pheromones that are used to entice us to make purchases in shops—the new science of atmospherics! Instead, as when most of us use the term, we are referring to how an environment makes us feel.[1] Physical places can often have their own atmosphere. Even if there are no people present, a school might feel friendly but a skyscraper threatening. A church building might feel sacred and/or perhaps welcoming. Some places can feel cold, even on the warmest of days.

Various factors contribute to how a place feels. These factors include the décor, the architecture, the lighting, and the temperature. To a certain extent, our sense of the atmosphere of a place is subjective. Memories are stirred up of similar places in our past, and the nature of those memories affects how we perceive the atmosphere of the place we are now in. Discussion about the atmosphere of a place is inevitably somewhat mystical. It takes us beyond the empirical and measurable, beyond the tangible and visible. As a result, there is not much research that focuses on it. But the capacity of the "atmosphere" of an environment to increase the feelings and experience of well-being has been recognized. A report published by the World Health Organization, for example, suggested that the most important single factor in treatment in psychiatric hospitals was the "intangible element which can only be described as its atmosphere."[2]

In applying the concept of "atmosphere" to salugenic relationships, we are taking the idea a little further than is often envisaged. Rather than talking about a physical place, we are referring to the atmosphere created by a group of people. They might be in a church building, a home, or a café—the geography is almost irrelevant. It is the atmosphere created by the relationships between them that is noticeable. Is it welcoming or cold? Does it feel safe or fearful? Is it peaceful or officious?

The atmosphere of a group of people cannot be created mechanically. You might have a church where every person is instructed to welcome the stranger, but this does not necessarily create a welcoming atmosphere. Likewise, you might be told that you are safe, but hearing the words does not create a safe atmosphere. You will know that you are in a salugenic community not because there is a sign on the door, but because the atmosphere is noticeably different.

"Atmosphere" and the Holy Spirit

So what is this "atmosphere"? We are suggesting that the uniquely different atmosphere that can be noticed by everyone present in a salugenic community is the manifest anointed presence of Christ through the Holy Spirit. It is the richness of His presence in our midst that is noticeable.

Scripture suggests that Christ sent us His Spirit in order to bring His presence to His followers, even though He was Himself ascending to heaven. The Holy Spirit, the Counselor, is said to bring from Christ a range of felt experiences, including comfort and strength (John 14:26); truth, or seeing things from His perspective (John 16:13); and, of course, power (Acts 1:8; 2 Timothy 1:7). Then we must include the fruit of the Spirit (Galatians 5:22–26) and gifts of the Holy Spirit (1 Corinthians 12:1–11). These will all make a significant difference to the atmosphere of any relationships.

It is important to note that we are not talking about a guaranteed emotional Christ-centered atmosphere that is present all the time. What we have found over the years is that in salugenic atmospheres the group is often not even aware that the Lord is present, and only later, seeing the fruit or outcome of the time together, do they realize that He had been with them. Think of the disciples with Christ in the boat during the storm (Matthew 8:23–27) or of Martha and Mary grieving for Lazarus before Jesus raised him from the dead (John 11:1–37). Even though Jesus was physically present, those experiences would not have been wholly positive. Yet God had a purpose under way, and it became clear, to those looking back later, that the event had contributed to greater wholeness in the lives of everyone present. The outcome added significantly to the history Jesus was writing together with His disciples. As they looked back together on what had happened and saw it from God's perspective, a new dimension was added to the atmosphere of the group.

On other occasions the atmosphere is clearly full of the manifest presence of Christ. Perhaps someone will have a confession, a declaration, a word, a picture, or a verse of Scripture, and everyone just knows that Christ is present. The disciples' experience with Jesus at the transfiguration was more like this (Luke 9:28–36). In the midst of the moment God revealed the truth of His Son.

These examples are based around Christ's physical presence with the disciples. In the contemporary church we have seen that Christ lives in us through the Holy Spirit. When we can each be present in relationships and carry Christ's presence, then the Holy Spirit in each one of us will create a new atmosphere through the perichoretic giving and receiving of our love for one another. Some may not know it is the presence of the Holy Spirit they can feel, but they will still be aware of "something" different. (We are very aware that we are touching on an area where much more thinking still needs to be done. We also admit that much of our own experience has been just that—experience. A theology of the presence of Christ in this salugenic way does need to be written, but this book is not the place for it.)

We would want to remind all our readers that a salugenic place, and its atmosphere, is Christ. For wherever one witnesses change, healing, or wholeness, one also sees Christ. But the form and atmosphere that are created by all these things merging will be different, even unique, every time. It must be that way, because God is present.

Some Complex Dynamics

Knowing that relationships become salugenic when they have an atmosphere full of the presence of Christ is helpful. We do not merely have to believe someone else's experience or accept Christ's presence "in faith." In a salugenic community we will each know on the basis of what we ourselves experience. This is the hallmark of salugenic relationships. But recognizing a salugenic atmosphere does not help us understand how this is created. In order to begin answering this question, we need to deviate slightly to consider a perspective that would have been quite comfortable to the Jews at the time of Christ but is unfamiliar to our Western empirically structured thinking.

In the modern Western world, where science is held in high esteem, most of us have unwittingly acquired a set of viewpoints and assumptions that are "scientifically" based. In *Trinity in Human Community* we describe how in Cartesian thought the material world is separated from the immaterial, the physical from that which is something other than physical. Although at risk of generalizing, it is relatively accurate to say that from a scientific perspective, something that cannot be seen is treated with a significant amount of skepticism. If it cannot be measured, it is often simply disregarded as if it doesn't exist. It is "merely" subjective and therefore is presumed not to contribute to knowledge. Spirituality has often been treated in this way.[3] The exploration of the significance of an "atmosphere" would certainly fall foul of this perspective.

Likewise, from a scientific perspective change is often assumed to be incremental, that is, measured and determined by a series of factors that can be individually identified and correlated. Even the academic discipline of social psychology, specializing as it does in the dynamics of relationships between people, relies heavily on artificially created experiments and their resulting statistics as its way of producing what it recognizes to be knowledge. The point is that these approaches will not help us understand how salugenic relationships can be created. Instead, it is more helpful to turn to complexity theory, a relatively recent rediscovery of some ancient concepts.

At its simplest, complexity theory suggests what many people recognize as being self-evident—that everything in life is connected and interrelated in ways that are complex. Also, that there is incessant change in every strata of our world. Rather than focusing on measuring things scientifically, complexity theory looks at the nature of the changes that are occurring and asks how we can better understand them.

When the Whole Is More Than Its Parts

One of the core assumptions of complexity theory is that the whole is more than the sum of its parts. Instead of growth being incremental (1+1=2), complexity theory explores those moments when 1+1 creates something completely different. It says that an outcome need not simply be made up of its core components. Some outcomes are much more than their original ingredients. Capra gives a simple example. At an atomic level, none of the components of sugar are themselves sweet. However, when mixed together appropriately, something different happens—the sweetness is created. Sugar is only sugar when it is whole.[4]

Here is the usefulness of complexity theory for our understanding of the salugenic characteristics of church life. The five characteristics that we have identified as integral to meeting Jesus together are each very significant. But when they are mixed together, something new begins to happen. There is a sweetness that emanates from the ingredients when together. We have described this as an "atmosphere." It is something that simply wasn't part of the original mix but has become very evident as a result of the blending of each element with the others.

Complexity theory calls this creative moment a "bifurcation point." Gladwell, as we described earlier, calls it a "tipping point." Christ's miracles are examples of bifurcation points. They are specific moments in time when something new is created that wasn't there before. One moment the man was lame; the next he was dancing. One moment the woman was condemned; the next her shame had gone and she was loved. One moment you could have eaten the ingredients and they were not sweet; sometime later they were sweet. Although such creation is not "ex nihilo," the outcome is significantly different from the original. The change is trans-formative, rather than re-formative.

Our observation is that moments when together we are significantly aware of Christ's presence can be described in this way. Too often the raw ingredients—ourselves in the group we are part of—are distracted, overwhelmed by the practicalities of the day, and absorbed in concerns unrelated to the group. Sometimes we are able to give the group our attention, although rarely from the deep inner part of ourselves that is the focus of salugenic change. Then, often suddenly and unpredictably, we find ourselves caught up in an awareness of the presence of Christ. One moment we were only partly present; the next we are deeply connected. The sweetness has come. There is a new atmosphere. It is what my (Susan's) PhD examiner recognized as "paradise."

The atmosphere of a group of people is part of the "whole" that is more than the sum of its parts. It is the extra that results from the combining of the ingredients. It is the consequence of a "tipping point" being reached. The sweetness of the presence of Christ enters the arena we are in, and we are aware that things have changed, or are about to change, forever.

When the Parts Become a Whole

Complexity theory has researched these bifurcation points in significant detail, especially in the natural world. Others are developing this research in technology, in business, and in the social world.[5] It is an exciting, emerging field.

One of the points of interest is, of course, how a bifurcation point is created. What leads to the whole becoming more than the sum of its parts? What makes a tipping point happen? When are relationships merely full of acceptance, safety, and openness? What happens to release that new atmosphere that carries oneness, that oozes the presence of Christ?

The moment before a bifurcation point takes place is known, in complexity theory, as a perturbation. Quite literally, the environment becomes "perturbed," disturbed. The normal patterns begin to change a little. Everything gets a little out of balance. For complexity theorists this is a clue that a bifurcation point might be coming, that there might be a moment of transformative change when something new will be created. There is a hint of uncertainty, an air of unexpectedness. The potential for something new to be created becomes palpable. Did the disciples have that experience? Could they tell that Christ was about to do something transformative, to say something life-changing? Certainly there were plenty of moments when the disruption He caused was not what they expected. Did they, perhaps, after some months of being with Him, begin to be able to anticipate these supernatural tipping points?

Of course, not all these perturbations lead to change. Perhaps the more familiar routines and circumstances prevail, the perturbation decreases, and the relationships between each part of the whole remain fundamentally unchanged. Jesus' encounters with the Pharisees were often like this. He offered something that would bring them the very thing they claimed to have made a priority in their lives. But they could not receive it. Sadly, we are often too successful at protecting our routines. Learning to live a life where we welcome such perturbations as signs that God is on the move and that transformative change is under way takes some practice!

However, there are also times when the perturbation increases until a bifurcation point is reached, the relationships between the parts of the whole fundamentally change, and something new is created. The shaking of an established pattern to create something new is a process that can be called "chaordic."[6] It is a chaos that is leading to a new form of order. The old patterns have gone. Something new is happening. In our personal lives these chaordic moments are the equivalent to discontinuous moments of change, the time when a new part of our Christlikeness is about to emerge. In a small group of people, the chaordic leads to a new atmosphere.

Chaordic change is, by definition, untidy. This is a time when the familiar sense of how things should be breaks down. It need not be in a particularly dramatic way, but it is certainly enough to be noticeable. Perhaps the amplification stops working midservice. No one knows quite what to do until several people in the middle of the congregation simply start to worship with their voices. Perhaps the person who has always led the small group bursts into tears. After an awkward moment of silence, the quietest member of the group shares a word from the Lord. Then there is a completely different atmosphere as everyone becomes aware of Christ's presence. Their attention is taken away from protecting themselves or meeting their own needs. The many become one in Christ—paradise.

Welcoming Chaordic Change

Can we make this type of change happen, a change where something new is created and there is a whole rather than simply a collection of ingredients? The answer is, "Probably not." If we were able to make it happen, we would be back in control again, managing things according to our own priorities and understanding because we do not believe God would cooperate! Chaordic change moves us into a place beyond mere change, to something different, more original than anything we had anticipated. We are speaking here of the transformation that God brings.

There is a lot we can do, and often do, to prevent chaordic change from occurring. Good management, ironically, can often obliterate the possibility of chaordic change by seeking to solve problems in a way that seems wise but is, in fact, obstructive. We tend to manage God's ambushes out of our programs, thereby avoiding surprises. Well-controlled and organized worship may carry a significant anointing, but if Christ had been allowed to interrupt, what might He have said?

If we want to welcome chaordic change, we will need to be prepared for those moments when things get messy and when we feel exposed and vulnerable. Our mechanisms for controlling the relationships and keeping ourselves relatively comfortable will have to break down, allowing a lighter touch from us. There will need to be more risk and more vulnerability when no one will quite know what to expect next. It is clear from an even cursory reading of the Gospels that this is what happened when the disciples were around Christ. The unexpected was the norm. Instead of spending much of His time smoothing things over, He put a great deal of energy into teaching and behaving in unexpected ways. So we should not be surprised that this is also what happens when He is in our midst today.

We should note that the outcome of chaordic change is not always salugenic. Interruptions in our routines can create a destructive sense of order, such as when a group of traditionalists steps into a leadership gap and imposes old ways instead of the more adventurous expressions of Christlikeness that the majority of the congregation had been seeking. Likewise, a new openness in a group can lead to division and abuse, rather than the deeper understanding and increased capacity to love that God had intended. For chaordic change to be salugenic, it must be in step with the other characteristics we have considered.

There are some in the field of complexity theory who are of the opinion that the outcome of chaordic change cannot be predicted or determined. They suggest that the interactions between all the parts of the system are simply too complex. In the case of human relationships, however, we would disagree. The intentionality of the members of a group, combined with the promised presence of Christ, can produce chaordic change that is salugenic in a more consistent way. It is still messy, but in that unpredictability participants find, together, more of Christ and each individually more of the person they were created to be. We call such experiences salugenic moments, and we will explore them in the next chapter.

Implications for Relationships

Complexity theory recognizes that when we are a group together, there is the potential for an added dimension that is something more than who we each are individually. This doesn't always happen in every group. We can each think of groups we belong to where the group remains nothing more than a collection of individuals. But—there is the potential for something more.

Think of an orchestra. You might have fifty or more instrumentalists, each contributing their own expertise. The rehearsals might be jagged and quite unharmonious. But in the concert there may be a moment when, perhaps suddenly, the musicians start to play as one. Melodies blend; harmonies complement each other; a different atmosphere is created. Instead of fifty individuals, you hear one orchestra. During the concert the audience feels part of the performance, caught up in the experience. The orchestra has led them on a journey into a new creative moment.

Think of the relationships between Father, Son, and Holy Spirit in the Trinity. Each has their own identity and makes their own unique contribution to the others. Yet each knows that they are incomplete without the other. They are three, but they are one. Their perichoretic relationship is a continual giving to and receiving from one another, each contributing to the mutual harmony that is who God is. They are never alone.

Because we reflect the image of the Trinity, our relationships with one another, in small groups and churches, have the potential to be like this. This same harmonious oneness is who we are in the body of Christ. God takes the individuals that we are most of the time and blends us into something far more harmonic, our own giving to and receiving from one another, something we do not normally experience. God has a challenge, for most of us do not do this naturally.

It seems clear from Scripture that God often strives with us to create chaordic moments when the individuality and false security and control of who we are, are broken down and a new oneness is unleashed among us. It is often when we are at our most insecure, at our most needful or vulnerable, that we allow Him to step in, in new ways. So in our relationships with one another, is it possible that we can welcome the disturbances, the change, the inconsistency, and the unpredictability? Can we together choose that when these times happen, we will each use them to move together toward more of who He has created us to be? Also, when such moments stop happening, can we stop and ask why and begin to invite God to step in and bring more chaordic transformative change?

To Consider

- Think of three different environments that form part of your daily life. How would you describe their "atmospheres"? What are the factors that contribute to that atmosphere?
- What were your most recent group situations where something unexpected started to happen? Was the old way of doing things reestablished, or did the perturbation lead to something new? Looking back, what would you have done differently?
- How does the prospect of chaordic change make you feel?

CHAPTER 19

Salugenic Moments

We are suggesting that the characteristics that support salugenic change are not enough on their own, just as the cake ingredients do not automatically make the cake. You may have a group that focuses on acceptance, openness, and choice, these may be the guidelines that frame the interaction of all its members, but that does not guarantee chaordic change. Likewise, there may be significant resources in the group to support a commitment to journeying together, and these may offer a good foundation. But their presence does not automatically create that authentic oneness that we may be seeking together. What we are suggesting is that there also has to be an element of mystery, a joining together with the presence of Christ by the Holy Spirit, something that is beyond the control of any human being. Something extra, often something chaordic, is needed to create the tipping point through which a salugenic community becomes a reality.

When such a tipping point is reached, the difference is noticeable to all. There is a new atmosphere, something palpably different. What is happening now belongs to the whole, rather than to any individual member. It is an experience of oneness, a commingling of everyone into one another with the Lord, rather than the more sterile compartmentalized individuality that was there before.

In our ministry we have begun to call these elusive experiences of being together "salugenic moments." They are those times, sadly too rare for most of us, when the anointing of Christ is tangibly among us.

Something changes, perhaps after some form of perturbation, and we are together, maybe only for a few minutes, in a different kind of space and place. Such a moment is described in a variety of ways. Some say it is a connectedness; some speak of feeling overwhelmed with love. Others experience it as a taste of heaven, while for some it is a profound experience of a need met or a prayer answered. It will always be different for everyone, but it has Christ at the center, and in everyone.

We started this book with a description of a women's group. One moment the women had their guard up, not trusting one another. Placing an empty chair in the room was all it took to break the cycle that they were in. When they realized that Christ was present, there was a tipping point, and each one of them felt differently. The group was changed. They experienced a salugenic moment together. But such a moment was preceded by a moment of confusion as I (Susan) did something more chaordic, or confusing. Scripture has many such moments.

In this book we have argued that salugenic moments, encounters with the Lord, are something that we experience together in a way that we do not when we are alone. But it could also be argued that such salugenic moments are the hallmark of personal encounters with Christ and cannot be restricted to moments when we are together with others with the Lord. For when an individual meets the Lord four persons are present: Father, Son, Holy Spirit, and the person themselves!

Salugenic Moments in Scripture

Think of Jesus' baptism or the transfiguration. They were exceptional salugenic moments for Christ. God stepped tangibly into the material world and expressed His unconditional acceptance of His Son. The barrier between the physical and the spiritual was dissolved, and human mortality became wrapped in eternity; human frailty encountered supernatural reality. An atmosphere was unleashed, created, that was fundamentally distinct from any and all of the raw ingredients of the moment.

The life of Christ has many more such moments. What about the woman caught in adultery or the woman at the well? It's possible both were transformed by their encounters with Christ. Or think of the centurion who was so concerned for his servant that he pleaded with Christ and received what he asked for. His household would never be the same. Or let us go to the upper room, where Christ and His disciples are celebrating the Passover. The whole of human history was changed by that moment.

What all these moments had in common was a range of basic characteristics. They had acceptance, choice, and openness. Each included a step further on a personal journey of growth and faith, together with the resources to make that journey effective. In addition, they most often also included the chaordic, something unexpected and uncomfortable in the encounter. There was always the supernatural dimension that Christ brings, turning potential into experienced reality.

In a similar way there are plenty of salugenic moments in the Old Testament. They were often celebrated in song (for example, Exodus 15, and many of the psalms). Others were described prophetically, as in Isaiah 61–62. Indeed from the first chapters of Genesis we see the defining salugenic moment—creation itself. Yes, God has had numerous salugenic divine community moments without us!

In speaking from Scripture about these salugenic moments, it is also important to note that not everyone found Christ's presence or His ideas and actions salugenic. As we have noted already, the Pharisees found Him offensive at times. He broke their rules and questioned their understanding of the ways of God. He proposed changes to their priorities and undermined the power and control they had over others. Some needed to "demonize" Him to justify not following Him. They turned against Him, saying He was from the Devil. Anyone who has been in pastoral work may have been a victim of similar assault, and it can hurt very deeply. Christ Himself said that when He was with us in our midst, there would be some who would hate us in the way that He was hated (Matthew 10:22; Mark 13:13). This is particularly the case where people are not ready to receive more of the wholeness that Christ offers. Instead, they choose, by default, to stay outside the groups we are talking about in this book.

But Christ was never distracted by such people. Instead, His ministry was about creating wholeness. It was available for all those who wanted it. If He is in our midst when we come together, surely we should expect Him to continue to create these moments among us, by the Holy Spirit?

The writing of human history with Christ is signposted with such salugenic moments. They are the tipping points, the pivotal moments, the defining evidence that God has been present. Such moments are His hallmark, His footprint that He was the one who brought the change about. It was Christ who birthed what happened. We all need such moments. We need to be able to say, "If it had not been for the Lord intervening . . ."

Twenty-First-Century Salugenic Moments?

It is frightening to think of what would have happened if our twenty-first-century church leadership had had responsibility for the effectiveness of Christ's ministry. We may have tried to find Him far more suitable locations, advertised His presence, and on His behalf prioritized those who would benefit most from His ministry. We would have kept Him to schedule, avoided storms and hungry crowds, and disciplined the disciples privately rather than in public. How many salugenic moments would we have inadvertently prevented?

Many of us have experienced salugenic moments at significant times in our lives. This is what we may have known at a Christian conference or a special event. There is perhaps the occasional church service or group meeting that turns out to be remarkable in ways we didn't expect. But is that not the crux of the matter? With the exception of occasional, unusually large gatherings or those people remarkably gifted in ministry, salugenic moment are more like surprises than everyday occurrences.

Is that what Christ intends? We don't think so. Our suggestion is that just as the opportunity for salugenic moments was created wherever Christ went in His ministry on earth, so He intends such moments to be created when He is present in our midst. We believe these should be the norm for the Christian life when we come together in His name.

Imagine what it would be like if each time you met with a group you were part of, you knew there would be a salugenic moment as you met Christ together. Imagine how you would feel if there were a consistency in your church services and every week there was something salugenic about your time together. You may not know what that will be, but you have grown to expect it. Perhaps your group has been able to grow wholeness-creating characteristics in your relationships together, encouraging acceptance, choice, and openness. Or as you meet in Christ's name, you are even more aware of the reality of His presence. You have come to learn that there is a tipping point that you reach when through the Holy Spirit it is as if Christ steps into the room.

We have noticed in our ministry that there is a deep yearning in human nature for these moments. It is in such moments that we feel most alive, most fully human, with all the richness God intended when He created male and female in His image. Such moments are also the times when we taste something of the reality of who we were created to be.

But a further word of caution. Creating such salugenic moments is not formulaic. We cannot artificially engineer the presence of Christ or the life that flows so abundantly when His anointing is unleashed. There must always be the bifurcation point when something that was not part of the normal man-made ingredients occurs in our midst. Nevertheless, we should be in no doubt, based as we are on the promises of Scripture, that God fully intends to manifest His presence when two or three are gathered in Christ's name.

One of the ways God enables us to participate in His creation of these moments is through spiritual gifting. A word of knowledge, a tongue followed by its interpretation, a prophecy—these are some of the ways in which God steps in to disturb our tidiness and control and create enough of an interruption for us to be open to His anointing. Before I (Susan) put that empty chair in the room for the women, I had asked the Lord how I could help these women become aware of His presence. That simple anointed idea helped create a salugenic moment.

So why are these moments so rare in our groups and in our churches? We have a number of different answers to this question. In part, it may be because we have eliminated any expectation of God's supernatural intervention in our meetings. Or perhaps we have lost the ability to hear His still small voice. Or we avoid the exposure of the storm by staying more safely on the shore.

Perhaps part of the answer lies in the quality of our relationships with one another. Few of us are in relationships that carry such deep levels of "reality" that we can simply and spontaneously be the people we were created to be. Moreover, the obstacles we put between one another that prevent authentic relationships being formed will also prevent Christ from being known in our midst. In the next chapter we will look at what we can do to create greater consistency, but first, a brief word about those salugenic moments that are apparently not Christ centered.

Are Salugenic Moments Always Christ Centered?

So far in this book we have focused specifically on salugenic moments that are specifically Christ centered. By doing this we may have created the impression that they are only possible when Christ is welcomed. It is now time to review this assumption. One of the more surprising things about salugenic moments is that they can happen just as easily among those who do not know Christ, or those who are not intentionally inviting His blessing, as among groups of Christians. In fact, there are those we have spoken with who suggest that salugenic moments will happen more readily outside the church than among church members.

You can deduce, from the way we have described the characteristics of a salugenic moment, that it is not exclusively the domain of Christians. Acceptance, choice, openness—these are qualities of human relationships that many people are seeking both inside and outside the church. They are part of what it means to be human. Is it only possible to experience salugenic moments when you are with other Christians? The answer to that question is a resounding "no." God, it seems, does not reserve the miracle of the salugenic merely for those who know Him.

In a recent discussion about salugenic moments, we were given examples from a diverse range of settings. One man spoke of a salugenic moment on the golf course when he intentionally created a situation where he took the blame and said sorry to someone who he knew was lying. Because he had made that relationship safe for the other, when the two met again, there was a remarkable salugenic moment. A woman spoke of a network of academic relationships where folk from diverse faiths not having come together on a regular basis spontaneously formed a community of mutual understanding in which each member was supporting the others. A man spoke of traveling the world, finding salugenic relationships in monasteries, of a variety of faiths, and then of returning to the church to be disappointed at their absence.

During my (Susan's) research I found examples of salugenic relationships in business, in schools, in therapeutic groups, in small community groups, in bars, etc.[1] The list is extensive. In fact, my conclusion was that these relationships can be formed anywhere where there are people who want them.

In many of the descriptions of salugenic moments that take place away from any overt Christian connection, there are clear references to most of the features we have described. Our question is whether Christ is also present in these relationships, even though He hasn't specifically been invited and isn't recognized. These are not people gathered "in Christ's name," and yet many of the same evidences of His presence are there.

There is no easy answer to this question. From one perspective, the answer is "yes." All that is good comes from God and God is love, so where there is love, there is Father, Son, and Holy Spirit. Any relationship, therefore, that is salugenic inevitably has Christ present. These are relationships that are journeying, releasing life, and full of truth—so they are in some sense relationships that are full of Him, who is the way, the truth, and the life (John 14:6).

However, many of those involved in such relationships would not confess Christ as their Lord and would be uncomfortable if they thought the function of the relationship was to lead them to Christ. These responses may be based on their preconceptions and prejudices about God. But we know that God has given us free will. This would suggest that if there are those who do not want Him present, He would honor that request.

Perhaps somewhere between these two extremes is the reality that God is present everywhere and will bless that which is in His will. For instance, it is definitely in His will that humanity should find new ways of living in love and possessing more wholeness.

We would like to be able to say that there is a noticeable difference between Christ-centered salugenic relationships and those that have no consciously chosen Christ-centered perspective. So far, however, we have no evidence of this. Perhaps in the years ahead, as greater numbers of Christians begin to practice these salugenic relationships, there will be a clear distinctive. What is true is that Christians do not have a monopoly on the presence of Christ. There are many who do not know His name who experience the reality of His presence. Simply by welcoming that which is salugenic, they are welcoming Christ, because He is the agent of creation, and where there is more wholeness, there is more of Christ.

Salugenesis and Christ

Are salugenic moments ever outside Christ? If Christ is the agent of all created reality, then the answer is a resounding "no." Based on this, we would like to suggest an idea.

Bonhoeffer, through his "worldliness of the Word of God" theology believed that "wherever therapy is, theology is present. Helping that which nurtures selfhood is Christian, regardless of whether or not the name of Jesus is mentioned."[2] Oden built an interesting thesis around Bonhoeffer's ideas, noting as he did that a two-sphere thinking exists, on the one hand, within the church and, on the other, within psychological therapies. This two-tier thinking has entered the church, where we now make a distinction between "Christian" and "non-Christian"—suggesting that there are places where Christ is and that there are places where He is not.[3]

We agree with Oden that such thinking is false and shallow. Instead, and taking up Bonhoeffer's idea, we would suggest that not only all "therapy" but also all positive change in any of our lives is in fact Christ inspired. We believe, as Bonhoeffer did, that this is the case whether or not Christ is acknowledged. Christ has created all human beings to pursue this quest, so in our seeking to be more of who He created us to be, through the process of positive change, we are always being helped by Christ in the way that He intended.

On this basis, all knowledge, wholeness, and healing are Christ centered, whether or not we acknowledge this. And salugenic moments will inevitably have Christ in them, regardless of whether or not this is acknowledged: "He is before all things, and in him all things hold together" (Colossians 1:17). When we increasingly experience salugenic moments, then we would suggest that we are being helped in the way Christ designed us to be helped. We are all recovering what has been lost to us.

A good description of salugenic moments and their outcomes may be found in Paul's letter to the Colossians, where he says that it is God's purpose for His people that they should be "renewed in knowledge in the image of [the] Creator" (Colossians 3:10). What is suggested is that this restoration is toward becoming more the way the Creator intended we should be and that Christ is with us in this process to bless and prosper us in this journey, whether or not He is acknowledged.

Implications for Relationships

We are suggesting that salugenic moments should not be elusive. Encounters with the presence of the living Christ should not be occasional. Though we should never presume, or adopt the audacious stance that we can "summon" God, we should expect Him to be there to help us in our groups as together we recover more of who we should be. So there is much we can do to ensure that our relationships lay the foundation for salugenic moments to occur.

We think of the wholeness-creation that Christ is always involved in as something similar to a mountain stream. It's a stream that always flows, never runs dry. Its water is fresh, bringing life to everything it touches. From time to time, however, that stream gets blocked, perhaps accidentally by branches and rocks, or perhaps more deliberately by human misbehavior. Then the stream disappears underground. When the blockages are removed, when the gulley is cleared, the river runs free again. So it is our responsibility to remove the obstacles in ourselves and in our relationships that in the past have obstructed the reality of the presence of Christ being manifest in our midst through numerous salugenic moments.

To Consider

- What is your favorite salugenic moment in Scripture? Spend some time letting God teach you more about it so that you understand it more deeply from His perspective.
- What spiritual gifting have you seen exercised that effectively made those present more deeply aware of Christ's presence?
- What spiritual gifting do you want to welcome, and how can you start to practice it in your small group?
- Which of your friendships, though not overtly Christ centered, have had salugenic moments? How can you welcome these more frequently?

CHAPTER 20

In Summary

C haordic change can seem daunting. Imagine being part of a community where the one thing that never changes is that it is always changing! Yet people are constantly changing. Christ manifests His presence in different ways. The interruptions and surprises have that element of spontaneity that defies even the most responsible preparation.

Salugenic moments occur where things are changing, where there is growth, where there is journeying and, therefore, the potential for more wholeness to be created and possessed. But, of course, we have to remember that "salugenic" refers to God's understanding of wholeness rather than ours.

When friends took the roof apart because they were so determined that the lame man would meet Jesus (Mark 2:4), the owner of the building may not have been that impressed. That may not have felt very salugenic to him. But if he was caught up in looking at things from God's perspective, what a privilege he would have found it that his was the roof undone in order that someone in need could find more Christlikeness.

We are suggesting that God is far more committed to the whole than we have realized in our individualistically oriented Western society. Of course, that includes meeting each of us in our need and in due course endowing us with an abundance of the gifting that flows through His image in us. But His expectation is that we will take our place in the community, in the body of Christ, in the kingdom. For it is in these relationships that we will find more of who we were created to be.

When Christ moves among us in these communities of His kingdom, in this part of the body of Christ, then where will we focus our attention? Will it be on the individual ingredients, and especially on those specific ingredients that matter the most to us? Or will it be on the whole, that which is more than any of us individually? Can we be part of a group that mutually gives and receives, thereby allowing ourselves together to be "in" Christ, letting Him bring chaordic change to increase the whole and its parts? If this is what we desire together, then salugenic moments will increase in frequency.

Part 7
BUILDING SALUGENIC COMMUNITIES IN CHRIST

We move on now to focus on the whole—that is, on the salugenic community itself. What does this "paradise" look and feel like, both from our perspective and God's perspective, in our material world and in the spiritual world?

SALUGENIC MOMENTS CANNOT BE ENGINEERED. BUT JUST LIKE a football team determined to win the league title, there is a huge amount we can all do to make salugenic moments more likely. We are familiar with the biblical injunctions to love one another, to forgive, to be as little children, etc. We can remind one another of this teaching and perhaps even do our best to make our actions comply. But living these supernatural truths from the core of our being in day-to-day life is much more of a challenge.

To begin with, to live this way we each need to be part of a salugenic community; that is, we need to have a group of relationships we are part of that are effectively, mutually salugenic and have such a consistency of salugenic moments that the relationships themselves become salugenic. Then we won't need the pretence, the control, the habits that keep people at arm's length from what we are really feeling. Although these relationships can be formed with anyone, anytime, in practice, for many of us they are unusual and rare. Look at the qualities we described earlier. They are not easily achieved, and they certainly do not happen by accident. Salugenic relationships are intentional. They take mutual commitment to giving and receiving.

We have noticed that there are a wide variety of relationships that are effectively salugenic. The most obvious is simply that between two people. They commit to supporting each other in the journey into their own and each other's wholeness and to meeting Jesus together consistently. They may be part of the same church, friends from different churches, or perhaps belong to no church at all. Ideally every marriage should be salugenic, although that demands high levels of wholeness from both partners and is certainly not where most people start in their exploration of salugenic relationships. In a marriage, there is often too much under-the-surface damage for the partners to have the depth of authenticity required for a salugenic relationship. It may even be that the basis of the marriage could be undermined by seeking more authenticity than is mutually helpful.

More challenging than simply a one-to-one salugenic relationship is being part of a small group. Two people do not form a community, but three begin that process. Once you have three or more people, you have a multidimensional set of dynamics that is potentially even more chaordic than the dynamics between two people. Within a small group the control and comfort of each participant is reduced as authenticity increases. Small groups are perhaps the easiest way to start exploring salugenic relationships. They can form a "whole" in the way that two people cannot. We see this mirrored in Scripture, in the relationship between the Father, Son, and Holy Spirit, who together are a divine community.

On a larger scale, churches and other organizations devoted to journeys of wholeness can also be salugenic communities full of salugenic relationships. There has to be personal interaction between members, so there are likely to be networks of small groups within the larger community, and these do create a more intimate authenticity. But if the values are shared and the small groups know they are part of a larger whole, then the significance of the salugenic community is much greater. In *Trinity in Human Community* we included numerous quotations from the early development of our congregation in Deal, U.K. It was indeed a salugenic community.

As we have said earlier, God does not intend such salugenic communities, of whatever size, to be as rare as they seem to be. For anything that uplifts Christ will be on the Father's heart. It is a tragedy that so many of us want to be part of a network of such wholeness-creating relationships yet cannot find them. We hunger for the sweetness of that blending of ingredients, for that atmosphere that is full of the palpable presence of Christ. And it is not only those who know Christ who are looking for this "paradise." People from all religions and from none recognize that extra "something" that is present when relationships are transformed and a new whole is created.

CHAPTER 21

The Salugenic Place

I t is now time to focus on the most significant concept related to salugenic relationships. Let us return to that church or group we have been imagining. We have seen relationships becoming increasingly salugenic. We have also witnessed a number of salugenic moments.

Now imagine that such a high proportion of relationships are salugenic that all the relationships begin to be affected so that salugenic relationships become the norm. Imagine also that instead of occasional salugenic moments, they are occurring each time the group meets. Here is the beginning of the "whole," the oneness, where all the members know that they belong to one another. We have called this "a salugenic place."

"Place" is one of those terms that is used all the time, and when we use it, we all assume that we know what it means.[1] I was several years into my (Susan's) research before I realized the very profound meaning that this word carried when used by those from whom I collected data. A salugenic place is a place that is made up of relationships rather than bricks and mortar. But it is also a place that feels just as real as something built of bricks.

Experiencing a Relational Place

The concept is a simple one, albeit more intuitive than scientific. Just as there are physical places that carry certain "atmospheres," so there are relational places that have atmospheres. Instead of being built with bricks and mortar, wood or steel and concrete, relational places are created from the relationships people build together. In the field of human geography there is a recognition of the significance of relationships to our experience of a place. The simplest example is "home." A house is a home not simply because its design and architecture make it a suitable dwelling, but also because of the relationships that make up family life. Or think of your local coffee shop. If you are fortunate, you will feel welcome, and if you are, it will be because of the relationships. Even on your first visit, the relationships of the team behind the counter contribute significantly to the amount of peace you feel when you savor your latte.

Relationships also have a significant capacity to affect how we feel about particular places. Schools feel friendly if we were welcomed and were successful in them. But they are hostile if we felt bullied. Even the most drab workplace can be made fulfilling by the quality of the teamwork of the employees. Relationships change our experience of our physical world.

Networks of relationships, therefore, have the potential to create salugenic places in spiritual reality, places that are just as real as the physical places of our material world. Each hello can become another brick in the wall. Each smile can add a little cement. When you offer help to someone in need, perhaps you are adding a whole new extension to this relational building. When you laugh together, a relational room gets painted a slightly different, more positive color.

Paul used a slightly different illustration. He described all of us who are in Christ as being together in relationship as part of the body of Christ (Romans 12:5; 1 Corinthians 12:27). It is made up of relationships where we laugh together, where we cry together, where we meet one another's needs together. Each of us brings our own uniqueness to this body. It simply won't function properly without us. It has both a physical reality, in our being together, as well as the spiritual reality of our being in Christ.

Have you ever tried imagining the internet? It is now part of the structure of our society. Many of us have come to rely on it. We cannot imagine living without it. Yet it is entirely invisible. Where does it reside? Vast numbers of computers act as servers to this technological world—the equivalent of its bricks and mortar. Communication is almost instantaneous, geography irrelevant, and they make possible a virtual global community residing in virtual places. The body of Christ and salugenic places can helpfully be imagined in the same way.

A Place without a Building

The mystical thing about relational places is that they do not need buildings. But just as we still have a body, even when it is not clothed, so a relational place still exists, even if it has no body.

In the early 1960s there was a famous sociological study of a bar named Jelly's in downtown Chicago.[2] In one part of the bar the men came, made their purchases, and then left again. The service was polite, but there were no significant relationships. In the other part of the bar, the locals hung out together. They knew one another by name, met frequently, and shared life's deepest problems together. They were, in many respects, a salugenic place.

As a result of some unspecified crisis and without any notice, Jelly's Bar suddenly had to close. Now there was nowhere for the men to meet. However, the researcher made a surprising observation. Night after night, outside the empty building, all the regulars kept on meeting. There was no drink to buy, no staff to serve them, no cozy corner to occupy. But they were there regularly, for months. This was where they belonged. The salugenic place had survived. The networks that these men called home did not need a building.[3] Salugenic places are like this. They may perhaps be associated with a physical location, as Jelly's Bar was for most of its life. But the "home" of the place is not in its buildings. Rather, home is the relational network that the members belong to. This is what they identify with. This is what gives them the atmosphere they find so alluring.

Scripture has many references to places that are fundamentally spiritual rather than physical. Think of Christ's reference to the many rooms in His Father's house (John 14:2) or to His ministry of knocking on the doors of our rooms and waiting to see if He will be invited in (Revelation 3:20). Some of the contents of our spiritual buildings are for noble purposes, but some much less so (2 Timothy 2:20–21). We often read these passages through the framework of our individualistic viewpoints, but should we perhaps revisit these truths on the basis that such rooms and buildings are made up of relationships that are part of a whole, a salugenic place?

As I (Susan) write the draft of this chapter, I'm sitting in the house of a friend among the Californian redwoods, eight thousand miles away from the place where my local church usually meets. Yet I am deeply aware that this English salugenic place has no physical geography to limit it. Distance is not a problem. I am missed when I am not physically present, just as I miss being there. Yet in some mysterious way it feels as if I have not left them and, simultaneously, as if they are here with me.

Creating a Salugenic Place

Being part of the body of Christ is such a reality that perhaps we should begin viewing ourselves as together creating a salugenic place. In 1 Corinthians 12 Paul speaks eloquently of how we belong to one another, each contributing such an essential part to the overall body that it simply cannot function properly if any one part doesn't contribute. Any body needs each part to stay healthy and to keep on growing. Likewise, together we are a building that we cannot simply construct once and then leave standing. Unlike physical buildings, relational networks require an ongoing act of formation, just as the mountain stream needs a continual supply of water to avoid running dry. In this sense, salugenic relationships are never really finished but are always being built.

Our relational building will start to crumble when the relationships start to disintegrate or get undermined. Moreover, if we all become too similar, we will end up with too many outside walls and not enough internal decoration. If one brick starts to chip away at another, every other brick will suffer. (We will be looking at this need to keep the body growing later.)

So how can we create these salugenic places? What is it that we can do to build networks that have such a palpable spiritual reality that others will notice and, through them, know that we are Christ's disciples? To begin with, we can pray that God will manifest His presence in our midst. Such salugenic moments certainly create the potential for salugenic places to emerge. But is creating a salugenic place the sovereign act of God, and God alone?

Without wishing to be formulaic, our observation is that the consistent chaordic creation of salugenic moments in a community or group where the majority of relationships are salugenic will themselves create the potential for a salugenic place. If your service every Sunday includes that tipping point that creates a salugenic moment, and if the day-to-day relationships among your group are effectively salugenic, then you will have given God the room He needs to build with you a salugenic place.

A balloon is a helpful analogy. When you buy balloons for a child's birthday party, they really do not look very exciting. When you blow one up, it is transformed. It gains features that are captivating for children (and adults!). There is no comparison between the balloons you bought and the balloons the children are playing with. In fact, they are so different that they deserve to be called two completely different things. There is a space, inside the balloon, that is filled with air. Something magical happened when the air moved from being outside to being inside the balloon. It is an invisible space, now inside the balloon, that means the rubber skin of the balloon is simply a container for something else. Together the air and its outer layer are now the balloon.

Salugenic places are like this. We start with a group of people, nothing special in themselves. But they begin to form relationships. They open up a space between one another by numerous interactions that are full of acceptance, choice, and openness. As the quality of those relationships increases, so the space becomes more secure until eventually a salugenic place is created.

A series of salugenic moments does not seem enough in itself to create a salugenic place. Imagine a large three-day Christian conference. Several times each day there is a palpable experience of the presence of Christ, and lives are changed. It is certainly salugenic for all who are there. But perhaps there are few who know one another, and there is often little that is deeply authentic in the relationships. This doesn't undermine the remarkable significance of the event in the lives of those who attend. But the majority of those present are passive rather than active recipients of the anointing of God.

Contrast this with a much smaller three-day seminar. Several times a day there is again a palpable experience of the presence of Christ. Lives are changed. But this time from the first meeting each person present is expected to speak openly with others about their need, their dreams, their pain. Relationships, however short term, are expected to be full of acceptance, openness, and choice. The participants share in one another's journeys and enjoy contributing to the resources of the group as they tell their stories of immediate transformative change. The salugenic relationships, together with the salugenic moments, create a salugenic place, even if only temporarily.

Of course, in our local churches and small groups there is far more potential to create salugenic places. Salugenic relationships can be built over an extended period of time. Acceptance and openness can be earned and implemented more gradually. Perhaps we can even ride in the slipstream of salugenic relationships that others have formed over many years. We can each play our part in contributing our own spiritual gifting to the creation of salugenic moments when Christ's presence is clearly felt. Our oneness as the body of Christ is palpable. The "paradise" of the salugenic place is evident for all who want to see.

Day-to-Day Salugenic Communities

The kingdom of God is made up of salugenic relationships, of the experience of salugenic moments in salugenic places. Here, in these times and places, the reality of heaven breaks into our day-to-day lives. They have an element of the miraculous, the supernatural, but in a natural kind of way. They achieve more than can be hoped for, in a slightly unpredictable way, and leave every participant changed through each encounter.

There is no doubt that people yearn for these types of relationships and experiences. Many do not know quite what it is they are looking for. If asked, they could not put it into words. But when they come across an environment like Jelly's Bar, or when they are part of an orchestra that plays in beautiful harmony, it is something they come back to again and again.

"Community" is the sociological word most commonly associated with the type of relationship dynamic we are talking about.[4] It conveys the experience of attachment, security, value, and respect. There have been many unhelpful expressions of community, of course, but salugenic places can be considered the equivalent in the spiritual world of the most sought-after communities of our physical world.

Community was God's idea first. He—Father, Son, and Holy Spirit—is a social yet divine community. Of course we are lonely when we are not in communities. Being alone is simply not part of how humanity was designed to be, hence Christ's high-priestly prayer that we may be one as Father, Son, and Holy Spirit are one (John 17:11). This is who we were created to be: people who carry the community of the Godhead in our oneness with one another.

One of the most profound experiences of a salugenic community is when we meet together in the breaking of bread, Eucharist, or Holy Communion. This means of grace is clearly intended by Christ to be salugenic, evidenced by the number of Christians down through the centuries who have been moved and changed by meeting the Lord and others during this sacrament. Christ expects that we will have dealt with any obstacles we have in our relationships with others in advance, so we can be in oneness when we meet in His presence together (1 Corinthians 11:23–27). If we have good leadership, we will feel that we are all participating in this process of remembrance. For a few minutes we are all together in oneness as the body of Christ, focusing on Christ, remembering Christ, just as He told us.

Implications for Relationships

If our networks of relationships create something similar to a place in the spiritual world, then a salugenic place is a particular type of relational place: it is a place that creates transformative change, a place that encourages all those who participate in it to move forward on their journeys of wholeness, discipleship, and Christlikeness. It is characterized by its own unique type of atmosphere.

Salugenic moments and places stand as beacons of light in contrast to other types of relational places that do not carry the presence of Christ. When visitors step into this place, they experience something fundamentally different. It is just as tangible as stepping in from the cold into the warmth generated by a log fire in an open hallway. There is no mistaking it. This is a place where you feel safe.

This is the paradise my (Susan's) PhD examiner encountered simply by reading my thesis. It is the kind of relationship many of us seek and would love to be part of, if we found it and had the courage to participate. The church has the potential to live out the oneness of a salugenic place in day-to-day life. It can offer authentic community to those who have been created to be part of it. It can offer the experience of meeting Jesus that Jesus' generation had all those years ago.

Is this wishful thinking? Can we really build relationships of such quality that whenever we are together we know that Christ is in our midst? Can we live in such oneness that others will know there is something different about us? Can we grow in Christlikeness, together, uniquely, becoming who we each were created to be?

The answer from Scripture and our own experience is a resounding YES! What we are describing is not simply a well-researched theory or idea. It is something being experienced, in part, among communities across the world. Some are in the world of business; some are religious communities; some are local, social groups involved in sports, music, drama, or other hobbies. Were we to cast our eye across the spiritual world from God's perspective, how many of these salugenic places would be alive and well in the church? Are they perhaps less prevalent in our churches? This is something we must each play our part in rectifying.

To Consider

- What have you just read regarding "place" that bothers you?
- What salugenic places have you witnessed or had the privilege of being part of? What impact did they have on you?
- Can you imagine leading someone to the Lord as a result of a salugenic place?

CHAPTER 22

Releasing Safety and Freedom

Reading about a salugenic place can feel a little abstract. Its sweetness and atmosphere, though palpable, are hard to describe. Just like the air in the balloon or the virtual world, spiritual reality is invisible to us unless we look at things from God's perspective and He pulls back the curtain.

But we can now go one step further in exploring what it is that holds together the relationships that are the fabric of the salugenic place. It can be expressed in two simple but profound concepts: safety and freedom. Christ embodied both, but only rarely do you find them present in salugenic ways in the same group of relationships. We will look at each individually, but then look in more detail at the remarkable interaction between the two. When this interaction is healthy and balanced, you will be in a salugenic place.

It is important to remember that safety and freedom, just like the sweetness of sugar, are not present simply in the core ingredients. They are the product of synergy, of the blending of them all. It is a bit like deciding that you want to grow an apple. You can't simply take something that looks like an apple, feed and water it a little, and hope to get another apple. An apple is the fruit of something that looks very un-apple-like—a tree. Similarly, the salugenic combination of safety and freedom is the fruit of a variety of dissimilar ingredients, each of which must be carefully nurtured. It is simply not effective to say, "What can we do to make these relationships safe?" and then institute a policy, preach a sermon, or set up some relational guidelines. Freedom and safety cannot be strategized. They are both fruit that grow when the soil and planting are done carefully. Once the tipping point is reached in the growth of this fruit, however, the sweetness of the Christlike blend of safety and freedom is the result. A salugenic place is created.

Safety

Safety in relationships is an elusive idea, hard to pin down, and yet one that most people instinctively understand. We have found that it is most often described by outlining its antithesis.

Think of a typical group of people you might be part of or associated with in daily life, perhaps a group of work colleagues or fellow parents. For a few days, watch how they respond to one another. The first question to ask yourself is how "real," how authentic, you see them being. You will find that many such relationships are quite superficial, perhaps polite, but with little that is personal and little that steps beyond the very specific focus of the relationship that brought you together in the first place. These are relationships that are primarily task oriented.

What would happen if someone in that group made a mistake, one that everyone got to hear about? How would that person feel? How would the group respond? Perhaps there would be some talk out of earshot of the one who had made the mistake. Perhaps this person would no longer feel quite as accepted, or even be ostracized. Would it lead to others feeling more determined to avoid or hide mistakes of their own in order not to be treated in the same way?

What would happen if someone in the group suddenly blurted out a secret that they were quite ashamed of, something that broke the norms of the group? Here we need to draw a distinction between what is said and what is felt. In some groups there is a supportive and forgiving verbal response but an invisible emotional condemnation. In other situations the condemnation is more honest and visible, with people being far more transparent about their shock and perhaps even showing disgust. Sometimes the latter is easier to deal with.

The groups we have described here could exist in a wide variety of contexts. They often seem to be socially well behaved but are definitely not environments where people would say they felt safe. Of course, there are many more situations in which the lack of safety is very evident.

Often people do not even pay lip service to the fact that their rude and abrupt behavior, or their mockery, criticism, and judgment, might have caused any of us pain. Instead, the action is either ignored or talked about later in groups where it is "safe" to do so.

Many of our group environments have an artificial, manufactured form of safety. It's a safety that is made up of being excessively polite, of saying "have a nice day," rather than "sort out your baggage and stop being so rude." This safety would rather lull someone into a false sense of security than speak truth and provoke change. This is not the kind of safety we see in Jesus' ministry. If this is what safety is, then Jesus certainly could not be thought of as safe.

So let's be clear about the type of safety we are talking about. It embraces each of the characteristics we considered in earlier chapters. It accommodates the raw openness of being real. It allows a person to live in their uniqueness and still be accepted, to make mistakes and not be judged. It encourages people to change as they share in the journeys of those both within and outside the group itself. This is a safety that allows uncomfortable truth to be spoken but also ensures that you know that you are still welcome. It permits the type of in-depth relationship where it is safe to talk about the thing you are most ashamed of and to engage the deepest areas of emotion with others. Here there are no pat answers. Knowledge is experiential, embracing the whole of the person.

Despite the rarity of such environments of safety, the quest for them is widespread. It crosses barriers of age, education, gender, religion, and culture. We might express this desire in different phraseology and seek it out in different ways, but whatever country we are in, whether we understand the language or not, we will know whether we feel safe.

In our book *Church as a Safe Place* we suggest that each of us is called to be a safe person, as Jesus was a safe person for everyone around Him—that is, for those who wanted safety on His terms.[1] Salugenic relationships help create in us the capacity to be safe people because when we feel safe, we can put our energy into growing and loving rather than into coping and protecting ourselves from others.

Freedom

Putting safety to one side for a moment, let us consider the other characteristic of the sweetness of salugenic relationships. It can be expressed in the word "freedom," freedom, that is, to become more of the person we were created to be, rather than the person we currently are. For we all need to become more like Christ. Safety is the more relational dimension of the salugenic; freedom focuses on the dynamics of growth and change that are more personal and individual. Freedom suggests movement, exploration, and life. Let us take a brief look at its antithesis.

When we are not free to change and grow, we are being restricted by a set of actual or perceived barriers or boundaries that we are unable or unwilling to break through. We bring many of these barriers with us into relationships with others. They are rooted in our beliefs, our historic relationships, and our personal choices. They may be imposed by others or be self-imposed. Whatever their source, our freedom is impeded.

One of the most powerful inhibitors of freedom is other people's expectations of us. If we are expected to be a certain type of person, that expectation will create a restriction. Though we may choose to ignore the restriction, crash through it, and continue our growth regardless, the very existence of the expectation restricts our freedom to be who we were created to be.

In an atmosphere that is salugenic, the expectation is that we will change and grow and continue journeying. It is assumed that we will take personal responsibility for this process and have the freedom to exercise our own choice in the direction and pace of that journey. Indeed, the atmosphere provokes that freedom in us, playing its part in propelling us into more of the person we are needing to become in Christ.

Another inhibitor of freedom is the inability to "be real." The type of freedom that is part of salugenic relationships is a freedom that has a depth of personal authenticity. It connects with the core of our being, however messy and chaotic. It engages our passion and requires that we participate holistically. It means that as people we are fully present in any situation, bringing the whole of ourselves.

Sadly, in many of the environments in which we find ourselves we are restricted to bringing simply that part of us that is most relevant to the context or purpose of the situation. In church we follow church traditions, in a therapeutic setting we talk about our damage, and in most employment contexts we have to fit in with the norms of the boss and their boss. Our freedom, or lack of it, is also made more complicated by the roles we take on in each situation. A teenager in a family will frequently adopt a greater measure of freedom, whether or not given by other family members. An established church member may have greater freedom than someone in leadership or someone who is a newcomer. Freedom is not distributed equally across an organization or in any other area in society.

As with safety, the type of freedom that is part of the atmosphere of salugenic relationships incorporates the other characteristics, the raw ingredients, that we have already discussed. Freedom naturally accommodates personal uniqueness, personal responsibility, and the making of mistakes. It must also respect the personal worth of others in the relationships, and it must be mutual: each individual must be allowed to be free, rather than freedom being the privilege of one person or group of people.

Many in our Western society have prioritized freedom at the expense of relationships and walk a lonely path, with limited success. Salugenic relationships offer the freedom of journeying combined with the resource of relationships to enable that journeying to be effective.

A Paradoxical Combination

We have described safety and freedom as the fruit of a salugenic atmosphere. As we look at this combination in more detail, it becomes evident why it is so rare.

When we think of an experience of feeling safe, we associate it with a sense of security, predictability, and an avoidance of unexpected change. Boundaries are established and respected, norms are shared, and there is a feeling of stability. Freedom is not something we most naturally associate with environments where we feel safe. Other people's freedom always has the potential to impinge on our own personal safety.

Yet safety that precludes freedom can be oppressive. It suggests that some one person, or group of people, has decided what is safe and that others do not have an equal amount of power (freedom) to choose an alternative. So some are safer than others. Safety without freedom comes close to a form of control, a paternalistic environment where some abdicate personal responsibility to others. It will lead to the environment becoming unsafe for some.

Let's look at the converse. In an environment where we feel free, there is a lack of constraining boundaries. We are empowered to make choices, and allowed to express our own uniqueness. This freedom also and often involves increased capacity to make changes and to be different. When we feel free to grow, to change, to make our own decisions, we will often not prioritize the safety of others and perhaps not even think about our own safety.

Yet freedom that is not tempered by safety can result in an undiluted chaos where the people who have the greatest capacity to exercise their own freedom trample over the freedom of others, thereby inhibiting their freedom. So in such environments some are freer than others. Unless it has clear boundaries, such freedom will destroy group life.

If a salugenic atmosphere depends on safety and freedom coexisting, here perhaps is one of the reasons why it is so rare. In the relationship between safety and freedom, each must sacrifice a little to the other in an ongoing negotiation of wholeness-creating environments.

The Fragility of the Salugenic

Unlike buildings in the material world, salugenic places are quite fragile. They are protected by quality, rather than quantity, experience rather than policy. They are the result of the contribution of the majority, rather than only the leadership. They also require ongoing creation and journeying, whereas a building, once it has been soundly built on a solid foundation, can be left alone. If we are to commit intentionally to creating salugenic places, we need to understand these dynamics. They have to be spoken about openly and discussed and explored when they begin to go awry. It is the group as a whole that keeps these in balance, not any one leader.

In our research we have found that the predominant aspect of the dynamics between the various characteristics of the salugenic place is a creative tension. Many characteristics have the potential to be in conflict with at least one of the others, safety and freedom, for instance, or shared journey and uniqueness. To be able to hold a balance between them all, so that each can contribute without being destructive, leads to a life-giving new freedom and interaction.

Think of two people standing, facing each other, and holding hands. Imagine that they both begin to lean away from each other. If they were not holding hands, they would both fall over. But if they get the balance right, they can each lean away and support the other. Now imagine a circle of people who are all holding hands. They all lean out, pulling away from one another. Now one person does not just rely on the support of one other person. It is the combined effect of all the group members leaning away from one another that creates the tension that allows them all to keep their balance.

This is one way of demonstrating both how a salugenic place is created and also how fragile it is. Each of the five ingredients we identified earlier—acceptance, choice, openness, journeying together, and enabling resources—has to interact with each of the others. They each pull in a slightly different direction. When they do so in balance, they open up a space where they can all interact in a healthy dynamic. But they each have to play their part in harmony and balance. When any one characteristic pulls disproportionately, the others tumble over, and the salugenic nature of the place begins to fade. For instance, perhaps "being allowed to choose" is asserted so significantly that the personal worth of others is compromised. Or the emphasis on acceptance might become so strong that there is no longer any desire to change and continue journeying.

These characteristics are not only in tension, of course. They also significantly add life and energy to the other characteristics. Being real is an acknowledgment of personal worth, as is holistic personhood. Mutual acceptance and participation are part of the common goal, while making mistakes combines with evidence of success to support the process of a changing community.

Another danger is that one characteristic may become a little warped, losing its integrity. Perhaps uniqueness turns to selfishness or acceptance to people-pleasing. Perhaps journeys are imposed, rather than chosen, or resources dwindle rather than multiply. When the ingredients are distorted, the dynamic of the salugenic place fades. The Christian life is marked by these paradoxes. Death and life go hand in hand. It is when we give that we receive. Even the three-in-one relationship of the Trinity defies tidy, logical understanding. So we should not be surprised that the kind of whole that is created when Christ is present is also full of creative tension. No one element can stand alone. To the extent that it stands alone it is ineffective. Each value must carry the values of the other, while also being fully itself.

The same is true of every part of a salugenic community. Each must carry the life of the whole. The teaching and discussion, for example, must add dynamic to safety and freedom; the leadership structures mirror mutual acceptance, participation, and personal responsibility. Guidelines and policies need to make room for mistakes and yet also offer safety. Again, the quality of personal relationships will have to aid movement toward the common goal. The whole of the organization will live the values of the individuals within it.

Implications for Relationships

Most of us welcome the prospect of relationships that carry both safety and freedom. Together they soften the worst excesses of the other. They leave room for personal change without that change being at the expense of the other. Safety is a free choice, and freedom feels safe.

In participating in these relationships we are both the recipients and the benefactors of the combination of safety and freedom that we have been describing. As the recipients, safety is usually the first aspect of salugenic relationships to make an impression on us. It is palpable in the atmosphere. It helps us breathe with deeper parts of our being than we have perhaps experienced before. It melts the hardness of our hearts and soothes our fear. But in time we have to allow that safety to change us so that we proactively receive it. Rather than simply letting it wash over us, we take hold of it and allow it to influence the decisions we make about the way in which we are to participate in the relationships of the group.

We respond by laying down our masks and our defense mechanisms. As we do, we become the benefactors of safety to others. They feel safer around us as we are more real and authentic. They know that we have chosen to trust them, to let them go deep in our lives, which increases their capacity to do the same for us. As the risk taken is mutual, the safety grows.

Freedom is often a dynamic that follows the experience of safety. With the encouragement of others we use the safety we have known as a launching pad from which to explore hitherto unreached parts of our being, both those we don't like and those we haven't yet found. We can explore the potential of who we were created to be, knowing that any adventure that might go awry will not jeopardize the safety we are already enjoying.

As we take up freedom and practice it, we accept the discipline of learning how to do so in a way that still protects the safety of others. We experience for ourselves the salugenic power of the combination of both freedom and safety and increase in our capacity to welcome the freedom of others, no longer fearing its impact on ourselves. We grow the capacity to love them and be one with them, while encouraging them to become the people they were uniquely created to be, rather than the people we feel we need them to be. The foundation of this relational model is quite simple. Safety is liberating, while freedom is relational.

To Consider

- Which do you lack most of, safety or freedom, and what can you do to address this?
- How can you safely talk about the unsafe parts of each person in the group?
- Which characteristic of a salugenic place is most likely to have too strong an influence on your group?

CHAPTER 23

In Summary

S alugenic places are real. They are made up of the space between relationships, filled with such an overflowing of wholeness-creating interaction that homes and families and the body of Christ are all part of spiritual reality.

When you are in a salugenic place, you will know it. So you do not need to ask, "How will I know?" There won't be a sign on the door. It won't need to be included on the notice sheet or embossed on the coffee mug. All of us know when we feel safe, and we know when we feel free to change and grow. These are the times when we are most aware that Christ is present in our midst. These are the times when we are able to live in the daily reality of the supernatural love that is the oneness that is Christ in us, expressed through our perichoretic giving and receiving. And because of this, these are the times when the world will know that we are His disciples.

But salugenic places cannot be created by rules. They will not be suitable for replication or for mass production. Simply going through a regular routine that is intended to induce trust will not automatically produce safety. Our man-made shortcuts and routines are not the fabric from which salugenic places are made.

There simply is no substitute for relationship building—relationships that carry a depth of authenticity, that primarily are experiential. These are the raw materials of salugenic places. When the chaordic is added, so that there is ongoing change full of salugenic moments, then people will notice that something different is going on.

Part 8

BECOMING PART OF THE BODY OF CHRIST

The whole that is the salugenic place is welcoming to those who want to be part of it. But once again we are not looking at a superficial process of attending meetings, even if that is a very regular and committed attendance. Joining a salugenic place means becoming a part of it. So how does this work?

SO FAR IN OUR EXPLORATION OF SALUGENIC COMMUNITY WE have looked at the processes of transformative change and also at the characteristics of the community itself. We have explored how it is that this community experiences its own moment of transformative change to become a salugenic place. Now, as the penultimate part of our exploration of salugenic communities, we will explore the experience of someone who steps into such a community for the first time.

Sociologically, the dynamic between the individual and the community is a very significant one, albeit problematic to research.[1] We are about to explore the relationship between the potential new member and the salugenic place. To put it theologically, we are considering the experience of a person who is for the first time becoming part of the body of Christ, though we are primarily looking sociologically, rather than reflecting on conversion. We are considering the social process of someone becoming one with a group of others.

Scripture places high expectations on this process, and our twenty-first-century Western society raises the bar even higher. Think of someone who is accustomed to living life independently and perceiving themselves as an individual. Realistically, how can they become "part of" the body of Christ? We are not talking here about simply attending a local congregation. This is about their taking their place as a member of the orchestra, offering their own unique contribution, so that the whole is no longer complete without them. We are talking about becoming part of the living dynamic that is the salugenic place.

The question is not only why they would want to—that is hard enough—but, more practically, how any of us make the shift from being a single entity to being one with a larger entity, especially when that larger entity is made up of people like us, with all our flaws and failings. It really is quite a ridiculous expectation when you think about it. The institution of marriage, where it is simply a question of two people becoming one, is breaking down and dying out. How can we expect ourselves or anyone else to want, or to be able, to successfully achieve oneness with a group of others we don't necessarily choose or even like?

In our churches we come together on a Sunday and perhaps mid-week, but do we really feel we belong to one another in one body? If Christ were suddenly to stand among us and make us one, even just for a few seconds, what would happen? I (Susan) used to presume that this oneness had a kind of golden glow to it, a beautiful experience for all involved! But my experience is quite the opposite. I would anticipate quite a few allergic reactions from most of us if we were to try to embrace a oneness with others who are part of the body.

I (Peter) always knew I needed to change to become more like Christ, but no one ever told me I could not do it alone. This was mainly because they were trying to do it alone themselves. It has been a huge shock over the last decade or two to realize that we really do need one another to help us integrate into this body.

If there were a group of us successfully living in the oneness that is a salugenic community, we would have to consider what it would feel like for a citizen of twenty-first-century Western society to begin to join our group. Such an exploration would help us make this joining process easier and prevent us from unwittingly putting obstacles in their (and our own) paths.

CHAPTER 24

Choosing Whether to Join

Joining a group is a process that has a variety of meanings, depending on the type of group. Some groups simply are not open to most of those who might want to join, for example, the British royal family or a famous pop group. Their membership is tightly defined and controlled. Others, for example, a university or an amateur dramatics group, permit joining if the person meets a number of criteria.

Churches usually have a broader policy. They will encourage visitors as well as new members, perhaps even regular visitors, who are treated as members in all but name. There might be a number of conditions attached to joining, often related to faith and sometimes to commitment to other aspects of church life, for example, regular giving, but often these are straightforward since one of the implicit or explicit goals of the church is to increase in numbers, and specifically to bring in, through evangelism, those who perhaps would not have thought of joining.

First Encounters with a Salugenic Church

Our suggestion in this book is that salugenic communities are attractive. They draw in people who want to pursue journeys of transformative change. Just as Jesus drew the crowds to Himself during His ministry, so His presence in the midst of salugenic communities draws those who are seeking Him. If you need to change, that is, if you cannot remain the way that you are, then Jesus is the one to be with.

In a church that is a salugenic community, evangelism relies heavily on the supernatural power of God's love and the hunger of the individual. When people find their needs are being met in a safe community, that gives them the freedom to grow in Christ. Because of this there will be some who want to join. But even those who choose to walk away should be blessed in doing so, just as Christ blessed the countless numbers He healed and maybe never saw again.[1] They must also feel that they are free to choose to come back, if they so wish, at some time in the future.

We often fail to see that Christ healed everyone who came to Him and then let them go, with no strings attached. Some came back, while the rest just enjoyed the miracle of their healing, and He probably never saw them again. Can our churches live this way?

First encounters with a salugenic church will take many different forms. However in my (Susan's) research, I found that there are broadly three types of response. There are some who experience the atmosphere of the salugenic community and respond very positively. They see the transformative change, and the opportunity to grow in Christlikeness and are able to identify with it. They enjoy the reality of the presence of Christ when the community meets together. It meets a felt need, and they want to experience more. These people begin to experience the acceptance of the community and the reality of Christ.

Others step into the salugenic place and have a very different reaction. Perhaps they feel that they are not ready to live in such openness or are unable to connect with the inner part of their personhood. Maybe they are not looking for a journey of growth and change. These people also experience the acceptance of the community, an acceptance that respects their choice. They are able to withdraw from the community, and, because they have been treated with honor, they will feel safe enough to return at some point in the future should they so choose.

The third group is the people who continue to attend the meetings from time to time but do not seem ready to participate fully. They appreciate being welcomed and accepted but are not ready to be open or to disclose their choice. They remain slightly separate and certainly don't participate in the oneness of the community, but they don't withdraw altogether. We have called it an "ongoing attendance." Some would probably describe them as the fringe membership. They keep dipping their toe into the water but don't want to swim.

On the basis of the characteristics of the community we have described over the last few chapters, this latter group of people is accepted for a period of time. But they will need to respect the values of the community. Even if they do not start their own journeys, within a number of months others around them will need to feel that they still support what is most important to the community, rather than standing aloof and judging it.

Permeable Boundaries

The dynamics we are describing here are mirrored in what we see of people's responses to Christ during His ministry. There were some who embraced His teaching and His call and chose to become part of His community. We know most, of course, about the twelve apostles, but there were clearly others who were a part of that salugenic community, too (see Luke 8:1–3; 10:1ff.). Then there were many who simply were not ready to embrace His truth and His requirements. They went away (for example, Luke 9:57–62).

It does seem, however, that there were also a large number of people who came in that "ongoing attendance" category. They showed up when Christ was teaching, brought their sick, and perhaps followed Him on His itinerant ministry as much as they could. Christ welcomed them, accepted them, ministered to them, and waited for them to make their choices. By the time of the ascension there were at least five hundred who were present to say goodbye (1 Corinthians 15:6).

The values of a salugenic church are such that outsiders are encouraged, and movement in and out is accepted and honored, rather than being judged. Choice, openness, and acceptance mean that the polarity of "them and us," "insider and outsider," is minimized.

Sociologically, most groups are defined by their boundaries. Their identities are defined by those whom they exclude. A band excludes those who don't play an instrument, a sports club those who don't express an interest in the sport. Our observation is that a salugenic church has a more inclusive emphasis. Anyone can be in "ongoing attendance" if they enjoy the experience of being with the community. Likewise, anyone can then become part of the body, part of the community itself, by choosing to share in its values and dynamics.

If someone who has become part of the body, part of the salugenic community, then leaves, the loss is noticed. There is no anonymous slipping away. It is hoped that the person leaving is doing so because it is a positive step on the next part of their journey toward greater Christlikeness. If so, amid the sadness of their going there is a celebration of their ongoing change. There is the opportunity for mutual blessing, even in that moment, and it is very likely that in some sense they will still continue to be part of the community. Such deep relationships are not undone simply by a physical absence.[2]

There are times, of course, when someone who has been part of the community will leave because they have been hurt and the community has not been able to successfully resolve the hurt, or perhaps there has been a misunderstanding or a disagreement. Endings like this are more painful, less salugenic, and should, of course, be avoided if at all possible. If they are unavoidable, then all parties will need support in seeing Father, Son, and Holy Spirit bring healing and redemption for the loss to the body, as well as to the person who has left. In a salugenic place, there is always the opportunity for the person to be welcomed back. In our experience, there is frequent movement in and out of the community before minds are finally made up.

First Steps

Let us focus on an unchurched contemporary person who has just begun experiencing a salugenic place. Perhaps they have come along a number of times and found themselves increasingly, perhaps inexplicably, drawn to come again and again. They may realize what it is that they find so attractive: the open warmth of the group, perhaps, or Christ's presence. They may know that they urgently need to benefit from a journey of transformative change that will bring relief to their immediate circumstances. Or perhaps they just simply find themselves continuing to come back, without knowing why.

We are aware that many of the concepts we have been describing are a little abstract. It is hard to imagine the salugenic place with any reality when it is a place that has no physical presence in the world. So for a few moments we will use a narrative style to tell the story of a hypothetical person who might begin the process of becoming part of the body of Christ by joining a salugenic church. We have chosen to imagine this citizen as a man, rather than a woman. Our churches generally find it easier to be attractive to women, and as women are often more intuitively relational than men,[3] they find that the exercise of becoming part of a group is more familiar. Many of the problems women face in joining the body of Christ are similar. But we will comment on this later on.

We will describe a typical scenario that might happen in any church that is practicing some of the characteristics that are part of a salugenic community. Then, based on my (Susan's) research, we will draw out the key moments in this person's introduction to the relationships of the salugenic place, that is, the start of his journey from being an individual to being part of the body of Christ. In the next chapter we will go on to look at his ongoing life in the community.

Introducing Henry

Henry is a regular kind of guy. He has a wife and kids, and although family relationships have been tricky at times, they've managed to hold it together. He's a manager at the local timber mill, has been for years. He's got a church background but doesn't really relate to much of the theology. He attended church for a while but felt like he was just going through the motions, so he left. His wife and kids still go, and he attends occasionally.

Henry has few close relationships. He sees himself as fairly independent. He works hard, has one or two hobbies, and doesn't do that much thinking about himself or his own needs. There have been a few occasions when he's stopped to recognize that he would like more out of life, but most of the time his life is full of work and family commitments, and that's enough.

For the past few months, unknown to his family, while they're at church on a Sunday, Henry has been dropping into a different church. He doesn't talk to many people and doesn't really join in. But there are guys there who look him in the eye and say hello. Several know his name and remember him from one week to the next. Within the first few weeks, one had invited him out for a coffee. Although he didn't go, he appreciates the offer.

The worship and teaching, in fact, the general atmosphere, at this church feel different. It seems a bit unpredictable, and the program and activities vary a lot from one week to the next. Some people kneel; some stand; some are clearly quite excited, while others sit in tears, with someone next to them mostly listening. The diversity surprises him, but it still feels quite comfortable.

There are no expectations placed on him about how to behave. That felt a bit confusing at first. He had to make more choices for himself than he would have liked. But he's got used to it. Sometimes he sings; sometimes he doesn't. One time he walked in late, and that seemed to be fine. Someone even left their seat and came over in the middle of a song to say hello. They also came over at the end and again invited him out for coffee. This time he felt he could say yes.

Most Sundays one or more folk stand up and talk about something significant in their life that has changed them. One week it was a guy who was just about to start his PhD. He got a big cheer. The next it was a woman who described how God had taken away the shame she felt from being abused as a child. She looked so radiant as she talked about meeting Jesus. Then there was a couple who talked about how their marriage was failing, but how they had both begun to discover the reasons why they hated themselves. They said they had been dumping that hate on each other and had now begun to learn not to. The man cried as he spoke.

Then one Sunday a guy who says his name's Tom stands up, and as he talks, Henry feels like Tom's describing him. He's a bit self-conscious until he realizes that no one else notices. Tom speaks about being bullied at school as a kid, by other kids and also by one of the teachers. He describes how as a result he made a decision to become a more private kind of person, independent but acquiescing when he needed to. But then Tom discovered that inside him was someone quite different waiting to come out. And when he began to welcome the pain of what had happened and let out the person inside, he started to change in some significant ways.

Suddenly Henry knows that he wants to know more about this change everyone is talking about. A quiet hope begins to stir in him that things could be different for him. He's not quite sure what things yet, but maybe some of the dreams he gave up years ago can begin to come alive again. He surprises himself by wandering up to Tom and beginning to talk more openly about himself than he ever has before.

Reaching a Turning Point

What we have just described is a typical journey that someone will go through in beginning to join a salugenic church. Some people will take longer than others. Some will know their need when they arrive. Many won't discover their need until they see that change really is possible. But all have the potential to begin an encounter with the salugenic place.

Remember that we are speaking here of a place that has reality in the spiritual world. When someone steps in, they should notice that it feels different, just as we notice the difference when we step from shadow into sunlight. They will, in an intangible sense, begin breathing in its atmosphere. The salugenic place, the network of relationships, begins to impact them.

My (Susan's) research suggests that as Henry begins his encounter with a salugenic place, there are three things that begin to happen. The first is that he allows the acceptance that is in the environment around him to impact him. He receives it, does not fight it. He allows himself to drop his guard a little. Did this happen when he went out for coffee? Or when he allowed himself to sit down when most others were standing up? Or perhaps it was the consistent acceptance he witnessed over several weeks that meant he was able to let himself be accepted. Whenever, however, he begins to submit to the gentle persuasion of the salugenic place and allows himself to be accepted.

The second thing is that Henry begins to believe that change is possible. He has seen some evidence of it, heard it talked about in teaching and testimony. He has asked some questions and satisfied himself that it is real. Then, linked with this, there is that moment when Henry moves from hearing about change in the lives of others to believing that he could himself change. It's a response from Henry's spirit rather than his understanding. It comes from below the water line of his conscious self. But it also, surprisingly, motivates him into acting differently. In some ways, he feels these things before he thinks them. Either way, the truth, atmosphere, and perspective of the salugenic place are beginning to prevail over the difficult experiences of his past.

Receiving acceptance and believing that change is possible can happen in any order in a salugenic place. But it is the third thing that happens that represents the real turning point. We describe this change as "being me." It is the point when Henry is willing just to start talking a little about himself. He lets his guard down enough to be honest and real. He is beginning to be able to talk about some of his dreams (the "me" he wants to become) and also about some of the damage in his life from being bullied (the "me" he has become so far). At this moment of "being me" in the salugenic place, Henry starts to become part of the community. Instead of holding back, he allows himself to be changed by what he is feeling and, almost against his better judgment, follows his desire to be open and honest.

When Change Begins

The three parts of the process of joining the salugenic place were clearly documented in my (Susan's) research. Theologically this turning point should not surprise us. If this is when someone like Henry really begins to become part of the body of Christ, part of the salugenic place, for the first time, there should be a radical difference. Suddenly Henry is not alone. He is not simply an individual who is also a manager, a husband, a father. Now he is part of a network of relationships with Christ, surrounded by people who are committed to supporting one another in ongoing journeys of transformative and Christlike change. In such an environment, with Christ requiring this of him, Henry can begin becoming more of who he was created to be.

There are three kinds of change that we can notice when people begin to become part of a salugenic place. The first is that they will recognize the change and say, "I feel different." Often this is because of a new feeling of hope as a result of beginning to believe that change is possible. They may also experience the safety and freedom of the salugenic place in a personal way. They feel safe and feel "free to be myself." There is sometimes a lingering fear of the change that lies ahead. But this is not enough to deter them.

The second kind of change is in their relationships with others. They are willing to be more real in some relationships as they respond to the openness of the community. Knowing that change is possible means that there is a greater willingness to talk about the more shameful parts of themselves. They can choose a greater measure of vulnerability and are able to grow a deeper sense of trust.

Finally, and this is the most tangible evidence that someone is beginning a journey of increasing oneness, there is a sense of belonging. People start to feel part of the community. They are able to begin to relax. This is becoming their community. They have become part of the body of Christ, even though for them it is much more about beginning to connect with others. The body of Christ is more whole because of their joining.

Implications for Relationships

It is tragic that often in our churches we do not look for that moment when the person has had a tangible experience of becoming part of the body of Christ. We treat it more as a transfer of allegiance. We say that once they are able to declare that Christ is Lord, then that, by definition, means they are part of His body. Well, from God's perspective, they are, of course. But we don't believe that God intends that to be simply a declaration of faith. It should be the beginning of something much more than just a decision.

Our experience is that the church should be able to offer folk like Henry something much more experiential, much more visible: it should offer a safe place. If someone does not feel as if they belong to the body, then God has more work to do. It is probably work among the members of this part of the body of Christ and also work in the life of the potential new member. But the truth is that we should each be able to experience that radical belonging to, and being part of, the body of Christ.

There is a type of belonging that is common in many churches. It is our attempt, perhaps, at creating a substitute for what God intends. If Henry were to begin to be part of such a congregation, he would be invited to participate in activities. Perhaps he would join the Sunday school or a midweek group. Maybe he would serve refreshments or move chairs. He would know that he belonged because one of the duties wouldn't get done if he were not there.

We are, we know, being slightly cynical and in some ways are overstating the case. But often our sense of belonging is based on what we can give and do rather than who we are. We would like to suggest, by contrast, that being part of the body of Christ is achieved in our personhood and wider relationships and that activity and service do not necessarily have to follow. We need to be aware of the radical significance of being willing to allow oneself to become part of the body of Christ, to move from independence to interdependence.

CHAPTER 25

Participation in the Salugenic Place

Joining, becoming part of the body of Christ is only the first step, of course. Now that Henry knows that he belongs and knows that change is possible, what happens next?

It is too easy, when a church has new members, to simply add them to the list and put them to work. We too often fail in our responsibility to disciple new converts. We presume that those joining us who have known Christ for any length of time will have few needs. If they are willing to share some of the responsibilities in the church, as an expression of their service, and if they are willing to tithe, then . . . job done! Of course, that is putting it a little extremely, maybe a little too bluntly, but sadly, sometimes, it is not so far from the truth.

It is hardly surprising that church begins to feel like an organization, rather than a living body of people who belong to one another. Of course, after a while, boredom will begin to set in. This was the surprising result of the research conducted at Willow Creek. Those who were most experienced were also those who were entertaining the possibility of leaving.[1] It may take some of us three years, and some thirty years, but eventually Henry, if he had joined such a church, would have begun wanting something more. Or perhaps, if not something more, then simply something different.

The reality is that God does not expect us to be satisfied with one moment of change at the beginning of our Christian life. Growth in Christlikeness is a change process, which continues throughout our lives.

As we have already said, transformative change is an ongoing process of becoming more of the people we were created to be. So how does the salugenic place support Henry in his adventure of continual becoming in Christ?

Henry Becomes Part of the body

Henry has been at this church for some six months. It's been quite a journey. When he first started talking to one or two guys about how his brother had bullied him, he had no idea where it would lead. It really wasn't any big deal, he thought. He'd just got used to it and learned how to avoid doing things that triggered his brother's animosity. So imagine his surprise and confusion when he discovered that others thought the behavior of his brother was really not what God had intended. Henry had been abused but had never admitted it.

Henry begins going to a men's group with the guy he'd gone out to coffee with and Tom, who had given the testimony. To his surprise he finds that even the guys who seem most established have things they want to sort out with God and one another. Everyone seems to be on a journey, and they all do it together. He finds this group a bit embarrassing at first because they all talk openly and there's a depth of feeling that's quite passionate, but these meetings quickly become the most refreshing times of his week.

The first time he gets angry about what happened to him as a kid is a shock to him. He's surprised how much pain he's been hiding and denying. Also, he would never have dared to think that his opinion about his brother would be allowed. To discover he feels so strongly is like meeting a part of himself he never guessed was there. But he's seen other guys do it, and it gives him permission to dare to be that honest himself. To his surprise, it even feels good to own it and let it all out. Afterward he's shown how he can give his brother to God and know that he won't have to apologize for himself the next time they meet.

But this journey that Henry is on isn't all about him. Some weeks he finds he's not focusing on any of his own "stuff." But he can really identify with how another guy feels, and finds himself getting absorbed in the process of helping him meet Jesus in his pain. Other times Henry finds himself reacting angrily or in fear, and the resistance he feels to any more change surprises him. Sometimes he even stays away for a week, not wanting to be around others who are ready to move on. This is not a problem, as they respect his space, but he knows it isn't really what he wants. He always goes back, gets rid of his attitude, and begins moving on again. At the end of every time together there is always a new sense of camaraderie. It feels like the evening has been significant.

One day the guys suggest he stands up in church and talks about when he was bullied and how, when he let go of his anger, Jesus helped him discover more of who he was created to be. That's a big step. At the end, there's a new guy who comes up to talk to him. He smiles . . . déjà vu! After that he's aware that in his group there are folk he can help, even while they help him. He finds out why it is that this community works without any officially trained leaders. Every member makes their own contribution from time to time. He has big dreams that are growing, dreams of who he can be, and maybe sometime soon he'll bring his wife and kids along, if they want to come.

Journeys of Discovery

Henry is typical of many folk who join a salugenic community. Some of us already know of major areas of damage in our lives before we join and begin the journey. But many of us simply know that we'd like more out of life and feel that there is something missing in our relationship with God and perhaps others.

Through our contact with others who are doing their own journeys of wholeness, we discover there are two parts to our journey of discovery. First, just as Henry discovered that the damage from the bullying was worse than he had admitted, so each of us discovers the parts of us that are not the way God created them to be. When Jesus is present, He wants to draw these things into the open. When we can see them, then we can seek out God's cleansing and redemption.

As background to this, we teach that all of us are profoundly damaged by a disease called sin and that we have more baggage and sin than we are prepared to admit. We also teach that from God's perspective He is more eager to talk to us about it than we are willing to make ourselves vulnerable enough to listen. So unlike many, we do not see two types of Christian, the successful and those who have failed in life. Instead, we see that all of us are the same. It is just that some can muddle along and provide for themselves, while others, at times, are not able to. If we were each to see ourselves from God's perspective, we would realize how far short we come of the people we have been created to be. It would spur us all on, together, in a journey of becoming more like Christ.

There is no detail of our history that is too small for God's attention. He wants to clean out, redecorate, and furnish every room of our spiritual house so that we and He can be fully present in it. That means He will have much to show us about how far we have strayed and how deeply we have been affected by the sin that we have often simply excused—that of others as well as our own.

From Wholeness to Mission

The second part of our journey of discovery is exploring the possibilities of who we are to become that we had previously been unable even to hope for. As we see others moving forward to dream bigger dreams, so their success becomes our hope that we may possess more of our future. None of us can imagine how much more God wants to give us, but as we journey with others, He will use them to introduce to us more of that potential.

This potential includes the growth of our spiritual gifting, our calling, and our own natural skills. This may mean education and training or pursuing new opportunities and responsibilities, within the church and outside. God wants to work throughout the whole of our lives to bring a oneness within us, as well as with others.

These two parts of our journey together in a salugenic community guarantee that the processes of change are ongoing. We will never arrive on our journey. Our attention should never be on any one goal. Rather, it is on the process of continual growing, continual "spurring each other on" into becoming more of the person each of us has been created to be. This unleashes more of the image of God in our lives, as well as the gifting and anointing that so many of us crave but cannot find. The journey is all about growing our capacity in Christ—how far can we go? Journeying in this way with others creates radically different relationships. The priority is helping one another move on, with mutual permission, provoking one another to possess more of Christ and carry more of the uniqueness of who we are. We discover the contribution we make to the lives of others, and they to us. We also discover more of the nature of God in the challenge of ongoing perichoretic giving and receiving among ourselves.

This ongoing change is captivating for all who bear witness to it. The change and its fruit speak loud and clear of the reality of the presence of Christ. It also is irresistible, drawing others on in their journeys, raising their own capacities to believe that change is possible—"I want some of that!" It acts as a resource in everyone's lives, becoming a kind of shared wholeness IQ that helps bring about the change God wants to unleash.

Participating

Over a number of months Henry becomes part of the body of Christ. It is a transition he first makes as he discovers that he needs these others to help grow more of who he was created to be. He welcomes what they have to bring him and allows himself to become vulnerable to them. Although he never realized it, in the past he missed out on letting others get close to him. It is a relief to be able to be real with them, to let them in to the parts of himself that he hasn't shared with anyone.

Becoming part of the group takes a slightly different turn when Henry allows them to challenge his resistance to change. Instead of leaving the initiative to him, they begin raising things he isn't ready to look at. It is always with his permission, but rarely comfortable.

As we saw earlier, one of Henry's most significant steps in becoming part of the community was when he was willing to give his own testimony for the first time and had a conversation with someone who wanted his help. It was then that he found he was able to give back something of what he had himself been given. Salugenic communities rely on every member being willing to do this. Each has their own story, their own expertise, gained by the experience of the journey they have been on. Henry's story becomes a resource for those others just beginning.

The process of becoming part of the whole is made up of many different steps, of course. Each of us has to take responsibility for our own significant contribution and begin bringing to every gathering the potential of who we were created to be. In time others can begin to rely on who we are, and similarly we learn to rely on them. Together we know that we are a community, ready to reach out to those potential members who are gently exploring the possibility of joining.

Salugenic places are maintained by ongoing giving and receiving among the relationships of their members. This intentional involvement on the part of each person is what keeps the place alive. This is the dynamic that forms the whole. There is a process of choosing to "give back" to the community as each member becomes more of an expert by experience. This fact is important, as it means that such a community is sustained by those who are "graduates" of the journey, and who are graduating, and not by leaders who are qualified to hold office in the church.

Implications for Relationships

Knowing that we are each part of the place we are creating in the spiritual world changes our attitude to one another. When we come together, we are more whole than when we are apart, and in leaving we take that extra wholeness with us. When we are not able to meet together, we know that the whole will be less because we are not there, and others will know that our contribution is missing. This is the clear teaching of the apostle Paul, but it is rarely a reality in daily church life. Living in salugenic relationship will make this New Testament teaching a palpable experience.

CHAPTER 26

In Summary

We should expect that becoming part of the body of Christ will be a challenging experience. Inevitably we give up a measure of our own independence as we become one with others. The church is more than simply an organization made up of people who share a common interest. The salugenic place has a living spiritual reality, expressed in our oneness in the presence of Christ. We are called to live out on earth the perichoretic dynamic of the divine community of the Trinity. Anyone beginning to take their place in that community will have a lot of adjusting to do. Those of us who already have the privilege of being part of this relational place have the responsibility of creating and preserving the permeability of the boundaries to mirror Christ's ministry. We have much to learn about how to raise expectations of the significance of becoming part of the body of Christ and how to support people salugenically as they embark on this journey.

Perhaps the most challenging responsibility, however, is that of learning how, as a salugenic community, we can each play our part. We have to maintain our own journeying into greater Christlikeness. We also have the privilege of sharing in the journeys of discovery of those in the body with us, both the cleansing of who we each have become and the growth of who we were created to be. Finally, we are called to contribute to the ongoing sustaining of the salugenic place, the living reality of the body of Christ.

Part 9

CREATING A SALUGENIC PLACE

This penultimate section of the book is specifically for those who want to begin to think about building salugenic relationships. We don't wish to describe the potential of all these relationships but then leave them out of reach simply by not being practical enough. So this section is optional reading—and is specifically for any who might want a little help in beginning the adventure.

IF YOU WANT TO CREATE A SALUGENIC PLACE, HOW DO YOU BEGIN? This is the question we have been most commonly asked when talking about these ideas or when people share their testimony about their adventures. There are many people who want to be part of a salugenic place but do not know of one locally that they can simply join. Our suggestion, if you find yourself in that situation, is that you start your own. Why not?

How many people do you need to start, sixty or more? Do you have to have experienced a significant amount of transformative change yourself before you can start? Do you have to be a "leader"? The answer to each of these questions is a resounding "No!"

We are writing this chapter for those of you who might want now or at some time in the future to start a salugenic community of whatever size. We will start by exploring how to start a small group that can become a salugenic place, and will then add a comment about how to apply these ideas in a larger preexisting local church.

CHAPTER 27

Choosing Salugenic Relationships

Let us imagine that you cannot see any small group in your current daily life that might become a salugenic community. You face two challenges. The first is to find those people suitable for you to be in salugenic relationship with, and the second is to know what to do when you begin.

Throughout the book we have sought to outline the key elements of a salugenic community. When you are looking for people to build a salugenic group, there are two elements or ideas that are immediately relevant. First, you must remember that salugenic relationships are mutual. Each person simultaneously both gives to and receives from the relationship. If some of you are more experienced than others, that is irrelevant. The mutuality of the relationships must be protected. You come as equals, each of you sharing a journey together. This is mainly about attitude, not "experience."

The second, and equally important, element is the journey you have in common. You are journeying together toward greater wholeness. Even though the wholeness that you each move into will be unique, it is a shared journey, and each of you is committed both to your own journey and to your shared journey. What you will be doing together is writing history of a type that is mostly new to all of you.

Finding Salugenic Relationships

You are looking for several others who share these ideas and commitments. We would suggest that you do not take too many other factors into account. The danger is that you will narrow down your list of possible people way shorter than those who are on God's list simply by excluding those for whom you think it simply wouldn't work. Share with one or two the ideas you have or give them this book to read. Then watch their reaction. Go for people you do not know too well. Invite the Lord to lead you to those who will be enthusiastic.

Be aware that God is not looking for those He thinks you are suited to! From His perspective, those who are quite different from you are going to have a far greater capacity to lead you in a journey to discover parts of you that you don't yet know even exist—both the unholy and the future potential.

Our suggestion as you start is that you stick with your own gender. This is particularly important while you are learning how to build salugenic relationships—adding in the complexity of gender distinctives is unnecessary and frequently unhelpful. Moreover, your spouse is likely to feel threatened. In a small group where you are meeting Christ together, it is all too easy for relationships between the opposite sexes to become unhelpfully close. You will also learn over time that men and women do this journey together in very different ways.

It is also our experience that starting off with your spouse in a small group will make your journeys harder for both of you. Relationships in salugenic groups are about transformative change. Getting under way authentically in this process of change is often much harder if there are people in the group who know you very well and are with you at home in your worst as well as your best moments. You are likely to constrain each other with expectations that are based on your history, rather than your potential.

Think of the people in your orbit who are the same gender as you. Which of them do you think might want to change, and which of them might value a friendship? Which of them might want to move on in their relationship with God in a way that is challenging and a little "out of the box"? Who has a need in their life that they are looking for help with? Perhaps a work colleague, a fellow parent at the school, and the most unlikely elderly woman at the church will all come to mind. Don't necessarily restrict your group to those who you think know Christ. Some of the safest relationships start off outside the church.

If you really cannot think of anyone with whom to build these relationships, then our suggestion is that you declare in prayer that you want them and need them and then see what God does. It is our experience that you will have surprising, God-initiated conversations, perhaps with complete strangers, that will be the clue that here there is some potential for salugenic relationship. You should expect this journey to be supernatural right from the beginning!

Meet for coffee, and tell the group what you would like to do. You can use this book to introduce the idea or simply talk about being in a group together where you can each support one another in growing into more of the people you were created to be. Set the tone for the group—be personal. Share with them what excites you about the potential for a group like this. Then see how they respond.

Don't take it personally if some say no. It will simply mean that they are not ready for the level of openness and accountability that a group like this will bring. You are not looking for a lot of people. Christ said it only takes two or three! Any number can work, perhaps to a maximum of six to seven for a small group.

As You Begin

Groups like this require two important elements to get them going each time they meet. One is ground rules; the other is willingness to be open.

It is important to have ground rules to help lay a foundation of safety. You need to know how you are going to treat one another. Again, you may find it helpful, as you start off in these relationships, to ensure that each person has read this book. That way you will know that you all have the same background knowledge and are speaking the same language. Of course, you can change any of the characteristics or suggestions in this book to suit your own unique community, but you all need to agree on the ground rules you wish to adhere to.

If you have folk in the group who do not have a church background, or who are not good with books, then you will have to find a different way to chat about the ground rules together. You will find simply sitting and asking, "What helps me feel safe in a group?" will produce many of the kinds of characteristics we have elaborated in this book.

Then you also need to begin to be a little open with one another. Talk a little more personally about yourselves. You do not need to make yourselves too vulnerable to one another as you start. That will grow as you get to know one another more deeply. But each of you, at each meeting, especially to start with, should contribute something about yourself, maybe simply by chatting about the type of environment you have left that was less safe, or beginning to talk about the change you would like to see in your life.

We suggest a small guideline. If you are someone who is comfortable talking in a group, then try talking a little less! If you are someone who is less comfortable talking in a group, then try talking a little more. See if gradually you can move to the situation where each person contributes approximately the same amount, averaged over several meetings.

Remember that your group is going to embrace the characteristics of transformative change. So together you will begin to connect emotionally, as well as in a more rational manner. If someone begins to weep, then you can let that happen. If someone is angry, then that is okay, too. There will be discontinuous moments when someone's contribution is radically different while they go through a time of change.

Remember, too, that the information that is shared in the group is confidential. It shouldn't even be spoken about with your spouse or with a friend as a prayer topic! But it is helpful to agree as a group that if anyone talks about something where the group feels out of its depth, you will decide together whose advice you might seek. In practice this happens very rarely, but it's good to know that you have agreed to get advice should you feel you need it.

Each group should agree how often to meet. Initially it is helpful to meet more often, perhaps weekly, since frequency is a key factor when we are learning new skills and building deeper relationships. Try to find a safe place to meet—somewhere where you won't be disturbed and where it is fine to make a noise. Someone's home is often the best, if there is a private room. Or is there a comfortable but private lounge area at a church? Basements of houses can be particularly cozy and soundproof!

The thing you can be sure of is that none of you will know how to do this before you start. This is a journey you will go on together and share responsibility for. You are expecting Christ to step in and meet you just as supernaturally as He did when He was present with the disciples. There will be lots of miracles, lots of chaordic moments.

The Change Journey

As we mentioned earlier in the book, we have specifically not looked in any detail at the process of change itself—that is, how it actually works. But we feel that for those of you who specifically want to start a journey together, not to provide any clues at all about the change processes might be a little unfair. So here are some suggestions to help you get going. You can mix and match those that are most helpful to your group.

Before we start our suggestions of what you might do when you are together, let us mention again that these Christ-centered relationships are a supernatural way of adding that ingredient that you feel is missing in your own journey of transformative change. This is a journey that each person in the group will be increasingly committed to. But we must stress that although much will be birthed in your group, the change process happens outside group meetings and then is added to by being part of the salugenic place. As a general rule, your group can expect each member to give some time during the week, outside group time, to the priority of their own change. When the group meets, this personal progress and effort become the raw material the Lord uses in the shared journey that you travel together.

Here are some ideas on what your group's journeying might include:

- *Meeting Jesus together.* The focus of the salugenic relationships we are discussing in this book is on becoming increasingly more aware of Christ's presence and on being changed by His presence and by what He says to us. So simply spending a few minutes welcoming Christ and letting Him speak to you all is very helpful. When you are together He is very likely to offer His own perspective on what someone has shared about their own situation. This must be welcomed and celebrated.

- *Welcoming and then letting go of damaged emotion.* Encouraging someone in the group to let emotion come to the surface and then, when they are ready, to give it to Jesus can be deeply therapeutic. (It can also be quite messy!) We often find that men's groups find this easier to do together earlier in the relationships, while women's groups will first want to build more trust.

- *Working on a specific topic.* One way to approach this is to agree together that at the next meeting you will each talk about your experience of something specific. It might be an area of damage, for instance, being betrayed; or of potential, for instance, an area of redemption you are seeking; or it might be a personal goal you are working toward. We suggest that during the week you each invite the Lord to reveal one specific thing that will help you move forward. When it is time for the next meeting, you will be amazed by what He has said.

- *Your spiritual house.* You might use the meditation in *Becoming More Like Christ* and each share about a room of your spiritual house where God is doing some cleansing.
- *Exposing shame.* You might each share the thing in your life that you are most ashamed of and then together invite the Lord to begin to undo the damage and bring deep cleansing.
- *Making declarations.* This is also a helpful way to spur one another on. Each person makes a declaration of the change they want to move into in the coming week or two, something very specific that can be measured; for example, has it happened or not? Often God will then use that as a way of launching a whole new agenda with each of you during the week.
- *Repentance.* Wesley used to start his weekly "class meetings" by inviting each member to speak out the sin they had committed since the last meeting. There will be times as a group when you will want to say sorry to the Lord, and to yourself and one another for the sin and damage in your own and one another's lives.

There are many other possibilities. God is the creator of originality and will ensure that He uses plenty of it in your group. Go to our website (www.lifegivingtrust.org), and share your experiences so that others can learn from them. There are also some additional resources there, and we would like to stand with you in your adventure.

Transforming a Church Salugenically

If you are already part of a local church, one of the questions you can explore is whether others in that church might also want salugenic relationships. Is it possible for your church to do this together? If it is, then how can you organize this?

Our view is that the answer to this question will be different for every church. The simplest answer is that in order for your church to do this together, you will need the support of the leadership and also of a majority of church members. This might happen over a period of time, or it might already be something that your church is actively wanting to promote. On the other hand, they may know nothing of this opportunity until you tell them!

Much of what we have talked about in this book can be introduced in teaching and preaching both on Sundays and in small groups. Familiarizing people with the concepts from a biblical perspective is very important. Many people respond quite intuitively and positively when they are presented with the ideas gradually, in a way that is integrated with language and concepts they are already familiar with.

If the church wants to explore these ideas, then form groups of equals, and follow the principles we have just described for starting a group. It is always helpful if some from the leadership are involved in these, but not as leaders. To start with, it may be easier if leaders meet in a group with other leaders. It will help avoid the temptations of leaders hiding in their roles and of others avoiding the risk of shared responsibility. Leaders must make themselves just as vulnerable as everyone else. In time, when people are more familiar with these dynamics, leaders will be able to participate mutually in more mixed groups.

Over a period of time, if your group meets consistently and follows these guidelines, you should develop a growing awareness of any areas of church life that are not salugenic. Perhaps there is a lack of unconditional acceptance of newcomers or an avoidance of the issue of difference and uniqueness in the women's work. Perhaps there are some who feel that mistakes cannot be talked about openly or that people's choices are not respected if they are unusual. There is often a lot that a church can do to make itself a safe place. We have written a book full of guidelines on how to do this.[1]

In addition to the church becoming a salugenic place, there will be a need for some in the church to begin their individual journeys of salugenic change. Perhaps the church may form several optional small groups, following some of the guidelines we have already outlined, for those who want to do this.

Gradually stories of successful transformative change can be shared on a Sunday morning. Yes, there will be many, and as they are shared more openly, people will begin to see the evidence of the change and, in turn, begin experiencing their own sense of freedom.

The combination of all these changes will begin to create the perturbation we described earlier, a change to the status quo. Salugenic moments will increase in the church services. Salugenic relationships will become more common. Members of the church will begin to feel they are journeying together into greater Christlikeness. A salugenic place will be the result. Christ will be among you doing what delights Him, restoring you individually and as a group.

CHAPTER 28

In Summary

All of us have the potential to begin exploring salugenic relationships. They are not easy, but they are life changing. Most of us begin with a significant amount of healthy apprehension. But as we meet Christ together and as we support one another in those many little miracles that bring ongoing transformation, we discover the reality of belonging deeply together as the body of Christ.

Do not be alarmed if the first salugenic relationships that God brings you are outside the church and are perhaps even with those who have no experience of a relationship with God. The relationship is still about you growing and changing in positive ways. You will see Christ present, even if others do not recognize Him. Your growth and transformation will be achieved, and you will grow in an experience of oneness with others that will also change their lives.

It is our belief and experience that God is passionately committed to supporting us in building salugenic relationships, communities, and churches. If we join Father, Son, and Holy Spirit in seeking such reality in our relationships together, then He is not going to fail us.

Conclusion
DISCIPLESHIP AS WHOLENESS

IT IS SAD TO NOTE THAT MANY CHURCHES ARE NOT SALUGENIC places. Likewise, it is tragic that when we are gathered in twos and threes we so often do not know the reality of the presence of Christ together with us. In this book we are suggesting that each of us can begin doing something about this problem by becoming more the vessels we were made to be, fit for the Lord's presence.

We each have a high calling. Made in the image of God, we are invited by Him to grow increasingly more Christlike as we discover who we have been created to be. We can live each day knowing Christ in us (John 17:23) and allowing ourselves to be consumed by the Father's love for the Son in us (John 17:26). This will require us to pursue a journey of transformative change, a journey that draws us deeper into the reality of God's presence in us, in others, and in His church.

The church, too, has a high calling. Just as Father, Son, and Holy Spirit are a social Trinity, so the body of Christ can mirror divine community. When we can love, we can live in the ongoing perichoretic giving and receiving that is at the heart of the Godhead. The world will know, as we live this supernatural love, that we are disciples of Christ (John 13:35).

Acceptance, choice, and openness need to fill our relationships. We must learn how to journey together and to provide one another with the resources we each need. As we do, the Holy Spirit will step in to bring us the presence of Christ in the kinds of numerous life-changing chaordic moments that characterized Christ's ministry and His life in us. When God moves in this way, something new is created. Instead of being a group of individuals, we become one, the body of Christ. Together we become part of a salugenic place. Were we able to see clearly, we would see a place in spiritual reality just as tangible as any building in our physical world, albeit that the salugenic place is continually re-creating itself by our ongoing journeying together.

When we have begun to practice living in these salugenic communities, we need to learn how to open their doors to the many who hunger for such truth and experience of reality. The shared journey of becoming more like Christ becomes contagious—we guarantee it. When we live in this way, everything about us will be transformed. Living salugenically will become a way of life, and it will have a particular impact on our capacity to live by the fruit of the Spirit, and to grow in spiritual gifting.

CHAPTER 29

Living Salugenically

We have talked about salugenic moments and relationships. We have explored salugenic communities, places, and churches. But Christ went one step further in His ministry. He lived, each day, salugenically with everyone He met, in all His relationships, in every situation. This is what we are all called to do.

Salugenic relationships change us. When we become part of a group of others, creating, sustaining, and growing a salugenic place, the life of the body of Christ is continually in us. Even when we are not physically present with this group of people to whom we now belong, we are still part of the salugenic place. The shared anointing that we carry is part of our daily lives.

The same is true of our journey toward greater wholeness. Our growing Christlikeness is the purposeful priority of our daily lives. Whether we have been Christians for decades or for just a few weeks, there is always more that God wants to do in us and with us to help each of us become the person we were created to be.

Part of the consequence of these relationships and this journey is that we will grow the capacity to live salugenically with everyone we meet. The type of salugenic relationships we have described in this book are mutual. We can be authentic and open with others when they are authentic with us. Our salugenic moments are shared together. But as we practice such relationships, something even more extraordinary begins to happen. We can move beyond the limitations of the mutual. We experience our own perturbation and begin to offer salugenic moments to those who are not yet able to return the honor.

Living salugenically means that we are able to use every moment, every opportunity, to create more wholeness, more Christlikeness, whatever the situation. As a result, we see situations transformed. Others will notice, but perhaps be unable to explain why they have found the conversation so significant. They are cut off from themselves yet still feel the wholeness stirring in them as a result of what we have given.

Imagine a marriage where one wants to pursue a salugenic relationship and the other doesn't. We agree that the situation is far from ideal. It is much better if both are able to offer this relationship to each other. But if one partner is able to be in salugenic relationships with a small group of others of the same sex, then over a period of time that partner will grow the capacity to live salugenically in the marriage, even if the other continues to be uninterested.

Think of a work environment. There may be only one person who wants to live in this way and allow these values to fill work relationships. Of course, the ideal is that a majority of folk on the team want to do the same. This would create mutuality. But if there is only one, this one can still live salugenically in all their relationships with their colleagues.

In fact, life becomes full of opportunities to bless others with the wholeness-creating reality of the presence of Christ. Families, visitors, casual acquaintances, even occasional contacts or complete strangers will know that something different has just occurred. It is what happened when Christ was physically present on earth during His ministry. It can happen again through His presence in and through us together.

Living salugenically is a supernatural way of life. And yet it is not reserved for that special category of supersaint we read about from time to time. It is an ongoing journey of growing and changing into even more of the person we were created to be in relationship with others.

Spiritual Gifting and Our Salugenic Journey

Living salugenically will necessarily involve our growth and maturing as people and will also introduce us to our spiritual gifting. Spiritual gifting and its anointing are one of the biggest needs in the church today. Few of us in the church have the power and anointing to demonstrate love and God's presence here on earth, especially not in the fruit and the gifts of God. Our salugenic journey is our path to this gifting and anointing.

The whole purpose of spiritual gifting is to manifest the presence of God on earth. It is gifting "for the common good" (1 Corinthians 12:7). It will allow His church to make Christ and the Christian life so incredibly attractive that they are irresistible—that is, to make them so real that others can believe and touch them as they touch you, to make them so priceless that actually nobody even thinks twice about following after you because they want what you have got. For you have learned that Christ is Himself irresistible on His own.

Moving into anointing and its spiritual gifting is nothing less than sharing God's perspective. All spiritual gifts are Christ's perspective spoken and lived here on earth. The anointing of spiritual gifting is Christ speaking to and through us. The sweetness of His love, the authority of His presence changes us forever because Christ did not come to earth to leave everything the way it was. Much He needs to change, and we are His change agents. What Christ needs from us is for us to change to be more like Him so that when we talk about God's perspective we are indeed speaking His heart and His mind. To do this we need to be on a journey of becoming more of who He has created us to be. When we know His perspective for ourselves, it is the most natural thing in the world to deliver it to others.

So there is a sense in which spiritual gifting is the grace of Christ bestowed on us in His honor, so that He can begin using us His way. We can then become more than our message, in truth, more than our life actually deserves. It is all about moving in spiritual reality with the knowledge of God's mind and His heart. Because we know, we then speak Christ to others.

God has given people free choice. Yet they need Christ, though they do not know it. They need God's word speaking to them, they need to hear His perspective if they are to live and to redeem who they should have been.

Spiritual Gifting and Suffering

Encountering the truth about ourselves from God's perspective is rarely pleasant. God does speak the most amazing truths about who He has created us to be. He gives us glimpses of the wholeness we are designed to live in. Yet such truth often merely exposes how far short we fall. As we have seen throughout this book, in Christ's presence sin is exposed. This salugenic journey into becoming more like Christ and living in spiritual gifting is therefore a journey that involves our growing and our suffering.

This should not surprise us. There is in Scripture an absolute dogmatic link between suffering for Christ and carrying spiritual authority and anointing for Christ, for instance, our need to go through the refiner's fire (Malachi 3:2–4), or Job meeting his Redeemer in his suffering: "I know that my Redeemer lives" (Job 19:25).

How do we volunteer for this suffering? We are suggesting that our journey into greater wholeness is the path Christ invites all of us to walk. We must be willing to go through the fires of refining, to lay on the altar of life all that is less than Christ in us, to openly declare what has secretly been hidden. Our more refined life becomes a vessel in His service. Suffering, our ministry's miserable message, is a means of grace whereby we are made fit for the Master's use.

Bonhoeffer wrote, "When Christ calls a man, he bids him come and die," and there is a sense in which we all need to become the living dead. Christ is a matter of life or death. There is nothing worth living for that isn't first worth dying for, and there is no greater death than to die in Christ for Christ. The salugenic journey is a dying for us, a dying to all that is sinful and all that from God's perspective is sin and baggage. It will be painful; at times we all want to quit, to turn against others and blame them for all that has happened and all that has not yet happened in our lives. But God does not demand everything from us without benefit to us. Christ will talk to us about our sin, our baggage, and its damage in our lives, but He will also talk to us about who we were created to be and who we are therefore becoming. One of the bonuses of our faithfulness in letting Christ be formed in us is that we learn how to live with a spiritual anointing and its gifts. For knowing Christ means we understand more of reality from Christ's perspective. Therefore:

- During the course of our journey, it is impossible for us to let go of the sin, disorder, and baggage in our lives without then seeing their damage in those around us. This can be the beginning of the spiritual gift of discernment.
- But as we learn more, seeing both the good and the bad that are in us, from God's perspective, as He talks to us, we will

begin to see others in the same way. This can be the beginning of the spiritual gift of knowledge.

- As we begin to believe that we have a personal calling and destiny in Christ, we will be able to believe the same for others. This can be the beginning of the spiritual gift of prophetic anointing.
- As we let the Lord teach us how to live righteously in our emotional lives, we will be more able to feel the passion of God. This can be the beginning of a deep, compassionate love for people and for the created world.

So Christ waits in the dark places in our lives. If we linger in nice, sunny meadows and pretty places, waiting to meet Him there, we are unlikely to find Him with any consistency or intimacy. If we choose superficiality and politeness, we are all in danger of losing the reality of His presence. He is God and He is always Lord, and He will not be manipulated. He came to redeem all that we have lost in our lives. If He cannot be Redeemer, if He cannot be Lord, then He merely waits to redeem in those places we do not want to visit in ourselves.

When you have been there yourself and seen Christ redeem what you have given to Him, you begin to earn the right to take everyone else there who wants to go. There is an abundance of spiritual gifting that can grow because we begin to see life from His perspective. But we have to go there first. Christ is waiting for us. Most of us do not meet Christ unless we are willing to meet Him as Redeemer, and we will not meet Him as Redeemer until we give Him something to redeem.

The greatest evidence of the power of the cross is our being redeemed by the Redeemer. But Christ cannot redeem what we will not own. Until we have seen it and admitted and confessed it, He cannot redeem it. If we won't let Him be Redeemer, then we will never know Him as Redeemer, for the gifting flows from what we know and who we then become. Turning up at church on a Sunday morning and saying, "I want the gifts," does not do it.

Many of us do want the gifts, but not the Giver on His terms. We want the authority and the anointing, but we actually don't want the journey to gain it. Spiritual gifting flows from a life lived and from knowing our God as Redeemer. So be willing to go to those dark places—because that is where you meet Christ as Redeemer. You will witness Him there as Redeemer in a way that is incredible, unimaginable, unbelievable. Such wholeness and redemption cannot be delivered by psychology or psychotherapy. It can be delivered only by God Himself. The Maker is the only healer and creator of wholeness in all of us.

So there will be many benefits to finding Christ in those salugenic places, but it will be about Him acting as Redeemer; it won't be about you. You will have all the gifting and all the anointing that you can handle, and then some. It is guaranteed because when you know the Lord in this way, you can speak His mind to others. When you bring God's perspective to those who are hungry for it, it will bring about permanent change in people's lives. They will never be the same again. They have been in the salugenic place with Christ.

The spiritual gifting can flow as naturally as breathing. But you first have to pay the price for it. You have to know Christ as Redeemer. Then you can turn to people and say, "I know my Redeemer lives. I can introduce Him to you, so He can do the same for you." You have been redeemed; you continue to be redeemed; you are seeing the Redeemer at work in your life. Telling others this good news is therefore really, authentically, easy. It is not a testimony from thirty years ago, for you are now living it at this moment. In seeing Christ being formed in you, you help others, by your words and your deeds, the fruit and the gifts. The salugenic journey will be all the suffering we really know in our lives, but it is enough for Christ to show Himself Redeemer and trust us with His toolbox to repair others.

Salugenic Communities—Journeying Together

In finding one another we find Christ, and in finding Christ we find new capacities to love ourselves and others. The suffering we are called to is not the life of the isolated, independent, very private saint. The redemption of Christ in our lives is not a private moment of glory as we meet Jesus in our quiet time. While significant, this is not what Scripture suggests should be the norm.

Instead, we are all called to a much more uncomfortable path. We belong to one another in Christ. We are part of one another in Christ. Each of us carries the gifting for another's journey into greater Christlikeness. Each of us brings more of the presence of Christ to the salugenic place, where all those present benefit.

When the Father brings us His love for the Son (John 17:26), this love will transform our communities. When we receive it, it is a love that cannot be quenched, cannot be silenced, and cannot be controlled. It will break down the barriers between us, unleashing a supernatural love that the world would not otherwise ever know about.

> My prayer is . . . that all of them may be one, Father, just as you are in me and I am in you. May they also be in us so that the world may believe that you have sent me. I have given them the glory that you gave me, that they may be one as we are one: I in them and you in me. . . . I have made you known to them, and will continue to make you known in order that the love you have for me may be in them and that I myself may be in them.
>
> (John 17:20–23, 26)

Lord Jesus, help us make it so.

The following is an excerpt from chapter 10 of our book *Becoming More Like Christ*.

Taking Possession of Our Spiritual House: A Meditation

We are going to imagine that you want to embark on (or continue) a journey toward greater Christlikeness. We will assume that you have accepted that this involves undoing areas of damage from your history, taking responsibility for personally changing in ways Christ invites. You want to enjoy greater salvation in your daily life, living in increasing holiness and wholeness.

Here is a meditation, based on the idea of the spiritual house, which you might find helpful as you begin to let the Lord teach you how to take the next steps on your journey. You are unique, so you will need to be flexible in the way you use this meditation. It is only intended to help you get started. Read it slowly. Stop at as many points as you wish to let the Lord talk to you, about you. You will need to do this journey with your feelings . . .

> Imagine your spiritual house. It was originally created by God but over the years has had a lot of wear and tear. You have invited Father, Son, and Holy Spirit to take their rightful place in your house. They have crossed the threshold and begun making Their home with you.

Your growing desire is for a greater measure of God's presence to fill every room, making it as it was originally designed to be.

Today you are going to approach a specific room. Which will it be? What door has the Lord led you to? What is the name over the room? It may be a person, a memory, a feeling, an area of sin, an event, or something else. Take time to let all the feelings associated with the name come to the surface.

Jesus is with you at the door of the room. He is encouraging you to open it when you feel ready. If getting into the room feels difficult, then ask the Lord to give you a key to help you. He may do it straightaway. Or it may be that the key will come in several days' time.

When you are ready to go in, the Lord will go in with you. He already knows what you will find. He comes with His light, His forgiveness, His mercy and love, His truth, His authority as Son of God. It is His intention to bring redemption and restoration to this area of your life so that this room can contribute to the growing wholeness of your life.

What do you find as you go into the room? A feeling, a word? What do you see? Is the room full of things? Are there lots of contents that you see? Or perhaps it is empty? Is there a draft blowing in from the open windows? Perhaps to start with you can't see anything? Take time to listen to the Lord talking to you about the room. Also, admit what you are thinking and feeling, preferably to someone else. You will probably discover you already know a lot about the room and the damage that it contains, but you are now willing to own or accept what you are thinking or feeling.

It is God's intention to help you clean up the room. This means He wants you to give to Him each area of damage that doesn't belong there. Perhaps it is an anger you have held on to for years, or the pain of a deep loss? Is it something you are ashamed of, or a word that someone said that has hurt you deeply? God is not in a hurry. He wants to do this job thoroughly so that you can know more of His redemption in this area of your life.

As well as asking you to give to Him each item of baggage in the room (usually one piece at a time!), He will want to give back to you those things that you have missed all these years. What does He want to fill the room with? Ask Him. He is often very specific. For instance, He will enlist your help in redecorating so you can grow in this area of your life.

Most of us encounter the problem of the house-maid, our intellect, when we are cleaning up these rooms. Don't allow yourself to think your way out of the room. Don't attempt to do the possessing and cleaning logically and sensibly. Remember that this is a spiritual house and God is doing some deep redeeming. Be willing to linger with Him. Expect both knowledge from God and His supernatural intervention.

Is God asking you to make some choices or repent of an area of sin related to this room? Invite Him to show you more. Let the feelings associated with the sin and the repentance be expressed freely as you welcome His forgiveness. Do you need to close the window to remove areas of unrighteous vulnerability?

When you are ready to stop, thank the Lord for what you have seen and what you and He have done. The dough is a little more kneaded today than it was yesterday. You may want to return to the room in a day or two's time, to do some more work. Or you may prefer to move on to another room and then go back to do more of this one some other time. Let the Lord lead you.

BIBLIOGRAPHY

Anderson, E., *A Place on the Corner* (Chicago: University of Chicago Press, 1978).

Bennett, M., and F. Sani (eds.), *The Development of the Social Self* (Hove, Kent: Psychology Press, 2004).

Bonhoeffer, D., *Ethics* (London: Touchstone Books, 1955/1995).

Byrne, D., *Complexity Theory and the Social Sciences* (London: Routledge, 1998).

Capra, F., *The Hidden Connections: A Science for Sustainable Living* (London: HarperCollins, 2002).

Clark, D., "Social Psychiatry: The Therapeutic Community Approach" in Campling, P., and R. Haigh (eds.), *Therapeutic Communities: Past, Present and Future* (London: Jessica Kingsley, 1999), 32–8.

Clinebell, H., *Basic Types of Pastoral Care and Counseling: Resources for the Ministry of Healing and Growth* (London: SCM Press, 1966/1984).

———, *Counseling for Spiritually Empowered Wholeness: A Hope-Centered Approach* (New York: Haworth Pastoral Press, 1995).

Erikson, E.H., *Childhood and Society* (New York: W.W. Norton, 1950/1963).

———, *Identity and the Life Cycle* (New York: W.W. Norton, 1959/1980).

Flanagan, K., and P.C. Jupp (eds.), *A Sociology of Spirituality* (Aldershot: Ashgate, 2007).

Gladwell, M., *The Tipping Point: How Little Things Can Make a Big Difference* (London: Little Brown, 2000).

Glaser, B.G., *Doing Grounded Theory: Issues and Discussions* (Mill Valley, Calif.: Sociology Press, 1998).

Glaser, B.G., and A.L. Strauss, *The Discovery of Grounded Theory: Strategies for Qualitative Research* (Mill Valley, Calif.: Sociology Press, 1967).

Glaser, B.G., and J.A. Holton, *The Grounded Theory Seminar Reader* (Mill

Valley, Calif.: Sociology Press, 2007).

Goffman, E., *The Presentation of Self in Everyday Life* (New York: Doubleday Anchor Books, 1959).

Hewitt, J.P., *Self and Society: A Symbolic Interactionist Social Psychology* (Needham Heights, Mass.: Allyn & Backon, 1976/2000).

Holmes, P.R., *Becoming More Human: Exploring the Interface of Spirituality, Discipleship and Therapeutic Faith Community* (Milton Keynes: Paternoster, 2005).

———, *Trinity in Human Community: Exploring Congregational Life in the Image of the Social Trinity* (Milton Keynes: Paternoster, 2006).

———, "Spirituality: Some Disciplinary Perspectives" in Flanagan, K. and P.C. Jupp (eds.), *A Sociology of Spirituality* (Aldershot: Ashgate, 2007), 23–42.

Holmes, P.R., and S.B. Williams, *Changed Lives: Extraordinary Stories of Ordinary People* (Milton Keynes: Authentic Media, 2005).

———, *Becoming More Like Christ: Introducing a Biblical Contemporary Journey* (Milton Keynes: Paternoster, 2007).

———, *Church as a Safe Place: A Handbook. Confronting, Resolving and Minimizing Abuse in the Church* (Milton Keynes: Authentic Media, 2008).

Maslow, A.H., *Motivation and Personality* (New York: Harper, 1970).

———, *Toward a Psychology of Being* (New Jersey: D. van Nostrand, 1962).

Melucci, A., *The Playing Self: Person and Meaning in the Planetary Society* (Cambridge: Cambridge University Press, 1996).

Miller, W.R., and J. C'de Baca, *Quantum Change: When Epiphanies and Sudden Insights Transform Ordinary Lives* (New York: Gilford Press, 2001).

Mitleton-Kelly, E. (ed.), *Complex Systems and Evolutionary Perspectives on Organisations: The Application of Complexity Theory to Organisations* (Oxford: Pergamon, Elsevier Science, 2003).

Oden, T.C., "Theology and Therapy: A New Look at Bonhoeffer" in Newton Maloney, H. (ed.), *Wholeness and Holiness: Readings in the Psychology/ Theology of Mental Health* (Grand Rapids: Baker, 1983), 199–222.

Quinn, R.E., *Deep Change: Discovering the Leader Within* (San Francisco, Calif.: Jossey-Bass, 1996).

Senge, P.M., C.O. Scharmer, J. Jaworski, B.S. Flowers, *Presence: Exploring Profound Change in People, Organizations and Society* (London: Nicholas Brearley Publishing, 2004).

Williams, S.B., and P.R. Holmes, *Letting God Heal: From Emotional Illness to Wholeness* (Milton Keynes: Authentic Media, 2004).

World Health Organization, *Expert Committee on Mental Health: 3rd Report* (Geneva: WHO, 1953).

Preface

1. This is my autobiography, written from the perspective of a number of principles I had to learn in order to cooperate with God's work of healing in my life. See Susan B. Williams and Peter R. Holmes, *Letting God Heal: From Emotional Illness to Wholeness* (Milton Keynes: Authentic Media, 2004).

2. Members of the congregation have given accounts of their own journeys into greater wholeness. See Peter R. Holmes and Susan B. Williams, *Changed Lives: Extraordinary Stories of Ordinary People* (Milton Keynes: Authentic Media, 2005).

3. Grounded theory was first discovered as a research methodology by Anselm Strauss and Barney Glaser. I was privileged to have Barney Glaser as an additional supervisor for my research. The original introduction to the methodology is found in Barney G. Glaser and Anselm L. Strauss, *The Discovery of Grounded Theory: Strategies for Qualitative Research* (Mill Valley, Calif.: Sociology Press, 1967). A more recent introduction is Barney G. Glaser, *Doing Grounded Theory: Issues and Discussions* (Mill Valley, Calif.: Sociology Press, 1998).

4. A summary of my theory can be found in Susan B. Williams, "Change-Enabling in a Salugenic Place" in Barney G. Glaser and Judith A. Holton (eds.), *The Grounded Theory Seminar Reader* (Mill Valley, Calif.: Sociology Press, 2007), 341–62. For a copy of the thesis and subsequent development of the ideas, go to www.lifegivingtrust.org.

1. "When Two or Three Are Gathered . . ."

1. Peter R. Holmes and Susan B. Williams, *Becoming More Like Christ: Introducing a Biblical Contemporary Journey* (Milton Keynes: Paternoster, 2007).

2. Becoming One

1. Peter R. Holmes, *Trinity in Human Community: Exploring Congregational Life in the Image of the Social Trinity* (Milton Keynes: Paternoster, 2006).

2. We introduce the concept of perichoresis in Holmes, *Trinity*, 29. We then develop and apply it further throughout the book.

3. Howard Clinebell, *Basic Types of Pastoral Care and Counselling: Resources for the Ministry of Healing and Growth* (London: SCM Press, 1966/1984), 110.

4. Clinebell, *Pastoral Care*, 110.

5. H. Clinebell, *Counseling for Spiritually Empowered Wholeness: A Hope-Centered Approach* (New York: Haworth Pastoral Press, 1995), 82.

6. This was the title of Peter's PhD thesis, Peter R. Holmes, *Becoming More Human: Exploring the Interface of Spirituality, Discipleship and Therapeutic Faith Community* (Milton Keynes: Paternoster, 2005).

Part 2. Transformative Change toward Christ

1. In *Becoming More Like Christ* we review this in more detail, acknowledging that in the Catholic tradition there is far more emphasis on the processes of spiritual formation (see Peter R. Holmes and Susan B. Williams, *Becoming More Like Christ: Introducing a Biblical Contemporary Journey* [Milton Keynes: Paternoster, 2007]).

4. Inner Change

1. Alberto Melucci, *The Playing Self: Person and Meaning in the Planetary Society* (Cambridge: Cambridge University Press, 1996), 61.

2. Hewitt offers a useful perspective from social psychology on identity formation. See John P. Hewitt, *Self and Society: A Symbolic Interactionist Social Psychology* (Needham Heights, Mass.: Allyn & Backon, 1976/2000). Personal identity can be interpreted as the sense of self built up as we embark on our own goals and develop our own autonomy (p. 98). It is the self as experienced personally by the individual and perhaps never revealed. See also Williams, section 4.3, in Susan B. Williams, "The Salugenic Place: Relationships That Empower Transformative Change," PhD thesis, University of Bristol (2007); available from ww.lifegivingtrust.org.

3. Peter R. Holmes, "Spirituality: Some Disciplinary Perspectives" in Kieran Flanagan and Peter C. Jupp (eds.), *A Sociology of Spirituality* (Aldershot: Ashgate, 2007), 23–42.

4. See respectively Robert E. Quinn, *Deep Change: Discovering the Leader Within* (San Francisco, Calif.: Jossey-Bass, 1996); Peter M. Senge, C. Otto Scharmer, Joseph Jaworski, Betty Sue Flowers, *Presence: Exploring Profound Change in People, Organizations and Society* (London: Nicholas Brearley

Publishing, 2004); William R. Miller and Janet C'de Baca, *Quantum Change: When Epiphanies and Sudden Insights Transform Ordinary Lives* (New York: Gilford Press, 2001).

5. Affects the Whole Person

1. Section 4.3 in Susan B. Williams, "The Salugenic Place: Relationships That Empower Transformative Change," PhD thesis, University of Bristol (2007); available from www.lifegivingtrust.org.
2. Holmes and Williams, *More Like Christ*, 100.

6. Relational Change

1. See my (Susan's) autobiography for more detail (Susan B. Williams and Peter R. Holmes, *Letting God Heal: From Emotional Illness to Wholeness* [Milton Keynes: Authentic Media, 2004]).

8. Discontinuous Change

1. See, for example, Mark Bennett and Fabio Sani (eds.), *The Development of the Social Self* (Hove, Kent: Psychology Press, 2004); Erik H. Erikson, *Childhood and Society* (New York: W.W. Norton, 1950/1963); Erik H. Erikson, *Identity and the Life Cycle* (New York: W.W. Norton, 1959/1980).
2. Malcolm Gladwell, *The Tipping Point: How Little Things Can Make a Big Difference* (London: Little Brown, 2000).
3. Peter R. Holmes and Susan B. Williams, *Becoming More Like Christ: Introducing a Biblical Contemporary Journey* (Milton Keynes: Paternoster, 2007), 132–6.

9. Choosing Christlikeness

1. Peter R. Holmes, *Becoming More Human: Exploring the Interface of Spirituality, Discipleship and Therapeutic Faith Community* (Milton Keynes: Paternoster, 2005), 83–93; Peter R. Holmes, *Trinity in Human Community: Exploring Congregational Life in the Image of the Social Trinity* (Milton Keynes: Paternoster, 2006), 86–109.

10. In Summary

1. See our website, www.lifegivingtrust.org.

11. Acceptance

1. William James is cited in R.W. Fuller's fascinating book on the damage we so easily experience in day-to-day relationships. See R.W. Fuller, *Somebodies*

and Nobodies: Overcoming the Abuse of Rank (Gabriola Island, BC: New Society Publishers, 2003).

2. Psychological perspectives that adopt the same assumption include Maslow's hierarchy of needs, Abraham H. Maslow, *Toward a Psychology of Being* (New Jersey: D. van Nostrand, 1962); Abraham H. Maslow, *Motivation and Personality* (New York: Harper, 1970).

3. See Peter R. Holmes, *Trinity in Human Community: Exploring Congregational Life in the Image of the Social Trinity* (Milton Keynes: Paternoster, 2006), 98ff.

12. Choice

1. In 2010 we will be publishing a book that explores a new model of pastoral care, enabling you to offer Christlike support and ministry without carrying responsibility for the person in need.

13. Openness

1. Erving Goffman, *The Presentation of Self in Everyday Life* (New York: Doubleday Anchor Books, 1959).

18. Creating an Atmosphere

1. Atmosphere is an elusive and intriguing part of group life. My (Susan's) research included an exploration of various ways of understanding this concept, including the conclusions put forward in therapeutic community literature, the philosophy of geography, and Japanese philosophy. See Susan B. Williams, "The Salugenic Place: Relationships That Empower Transformative Change," PhD thesis, University of Bristol (2007); available from www.lifegivingtrust. org.

2. World Health Organization, *Expert Committee on Mental Health: 3rd Report* (Geneva: WHO, 1953). This report is summarized in David Clark, "Social Psychiatry: The Therapeutic Community Approach" in Penelope Campling and Rex Haigh (eds.), *Therapeutic Communities: Past, Present and Future* (London: Jessica Kingsley, 1999), 32–8.

3. For a review of spirituality from a sociological perspective, see Kieran Flanagan and Peter C. Jupp, *A Sociology of Spirituality* (Aldershot: Ashgate, 2007).

4. Fritjof Capra, *The Hidden Connections: A Science for Sustainable Living* (London: HarperCollins, 2002), 36.

5. Useful introductions to complexity theory for the social world can be found in David Byrne, *Complexity Theory and the Social Sciences* (London: Routledge, 1998); and Eve Mitleton-Kelly (ed.), *Complex Systems and*

Evolutionary Perspectives on Organisations: The Application of Complexity Theory to Organisations (Oxford: Pergamon, Elsevier Science, 2003).

6. The term "chaordic" was first used by Dee Hock, founder and CEO of Visa International, to describe a new form of organization. See Dee W. Hock, "The Chaordic Organization: Out of Control and into Order," World Business Academy Perspectives, Vol. 9, No. 1, 1995, at www.ki-net.co.uk/graphics/Dee%20Hock%20-%20The%20Chaordic%20Organization.pdf.

19. Salugenic Moments

1. See chapter 13 of Susan B. Williams, "The Salugenic Place: Relationships That Empower Transformative Change," PhD thesis, University of Bristol (2007); available from www.lifegivingtrust.org.

2. Dietrich Bonhoeffer, *Ethics* (London: Touchstone Books, 1955/1995), 193ff.

3. Thomas C. Oden, "Theology and Therapy: A New Look at Bonhoeffer" in H. Newton Maloney (ed.), *Wholeness and Holiness: Readings in the Psychology/Theology of Mental Health* (Grand Rapids: Baker, 1983), 199–222.

21. The Salugenic Place

1. As part of my research I (Susan) drew up a typology of place, exploring numerous different types of place and space. It can be found in chapter 8, #6362, of Susan B. Williams, "The Salugenic Place: Relationships That Empower Transformative Change," PhD thesis, University of Bristol (2007); available from www.lifegivingtrust.org.

2. Elijah Anderson, *A Place on the Corner* (Chicago: University of Chicago Press, 1978).

3. After a number of months, just as unexpectedly as its closure, Jelly's Bar opened again. The men were once again given a building in which to house the home they had so carefully maintained.

4. I (Peter) have explored these ideas more fully in Peter R. Holmes, *Trinity in Human Community: Exploring Congregational Life in the Image of the Social Trinity* (Milton Keynes: Paternoster, 2006).

22. Releasing Safety and Freedom

1. See Peter R. Holmes and Susan B. Williams, *Church as a Safe Place: A Handbook. Confronting, Resolving and Minimizing Abuse in the Church* (Milton Keynes, Authentic Media, 2008).

Part 2. Transformative Change toward Christ

1. One of the most interesting and long-standing challenges of sociology and social psychology is the challenge to explore the relationship between the individual and the group, the micro and macro perspectives. Similarly, there is much we have to learn about the relationship between the individual and the body of Christ.

24. Choosing Whether to Join

1. In *Church as a Safe Place* we expand on this statement in a little more detail, suggesting that churches develop an exit strategy to bless those who want to leave! See Peter R. Holmes and Susan B. Williams, *Church as a Safe Place: A Handbook. Confronting, Resolving and Minimizing Abuse in the Church* (Milton Keynes, Authentic Media, 2008).

2. For our suggestion on what such an exit strategy might look like, see Holmes and Williams, *Safe Place*, 254ff.

3. We do not find gender stereotypes helpful. In our ministry we have developed the concept of the gender continuum to illustrate the uniqueness within male and female. See Peter R. Holmes and Susan B. Williams, *Becoming More Like Christ: Introducing a Biblical Contemporary Journey* (Milton Keynes: Paternoster, 2007), 38–9.

25. Participation in the Salugenic Place

1. See G. Hawkins and C. Parkinson, *Reveal: Where Are You?* (Chicago: Willow Creek Publications, 2006).

27. Choosing Salugenic Relationships

1. See Peter R. Holmes and Susan B. Williams, *Church as a Safe Place: A Handbook. Confronting, Resolving and Minimizing Abuse in the Church* (Milton Keynes, Authentic Media, 2008).

SUBJECT INDEX

SCRIPTURE INDEX

Also Available

The Fasting Journey—written by a man for whom fasting has become a way of life—is a journal of his experiences and a guide for those of us who want to learn from someone who has known firsthand the joys and hardships of fasting.

Peter Holmes shows us how fasting is a death of self and an act of intercession that God uses as a spiritual weapon to clarify and unleash God's purposes to bring about healing for those trapped in bondage to sin. Because of the understanding God has given him through fasting, he has helped many find answers to their most complex and deeply entrenched problems.

Holmes discusses the biblical aspect of fasting from Old Testament Scriptures to the practice of the early church. He explains different kinds of fasts for us to consider—even non-food fasts—explores purposes for fasting, and tells us how our fasting will impact those around us. In *The Fasting Journey*, we are called to fast as a way to find out what really controls us, to become more Christlike, and to hear God's voice with a clear, focused ear.

Retail: $15.99
ISBN: 978-1-60657-018-0

Available for purchase at book retailers everywhere.